The Sales

*The Difference Between
The Average Salesperson & The
Successful Sales Professional*

Chris Randolph

PAUL,
You're Awesome
Best for Success!
Chris Randolph

ISBN-10 1-60145-007-9
ISBN-13 978-1-60145-007-4

Randolph, Chris.
The Sales Edge:
The Difference Between The Average Salesperson And The Successful Sales Professional.

2006/First Print

This book is available at a special discount when ordered in bulk quantities.

For information, contact the author via email at chris@thesalesedge.biz.

Or write to The Sales Edge,
7964 Arjons Dr, Suite H-106, San Diego, CA 92126.

Or call 858-547-9195.

www.thesalesedge.biz

This book is dedicated to some very special and wonderful people in my life:

Swee, my mother, who raised my brother and I by herself.
Paul, my father, who passed on when I was 7 years old.
Yit, my beautiful wife, who stands by me through thick and thin.
Sydney & Patric, my daughter and son.
Daniel, my brother.
Mr. and Mrs. Hoh, my in-laws.
Herb and Lany Niederheiser.
Eric Payumo, a great friend.
Doc, who helped me see my purpose.
From the bottom of my heart, <u>THANK YOU.</u>

CR

CONTENTS

Introduction. vii

PART A: SKILL SET 1

Chapter 1: How People Make Buying Decisions 3
Chapter 2: Building Trust and Rapport 13
Chapter 3: Successful Prospecting 21
Chapter 4: Sales Scripts 27
Chapter 5: Referrals And Networking 37
Chapter 6: Power Negotiating Secrets 43
Chapter 7: How To Handle Any Objection 59
Chapter 8: Asking The Right Questions 67
Chapter 9: Closing Skills And Strategies 71

PART B: MINDSET 77

Chapter 10: Characteristics of A Sales Professional 79
Chapter 11: How To Set And Achieve Any Goal 85
Chapter 12: Time Management For Sales Professionals 93
Chapter 13: Overcoming Fear & Procrastination 99
Chapter 14: No Such Thing As Bulletproof Psychology 107
Chapter 15: Get More Done Using Feeling vs. Action 115
Chapter 16: BONUS 25 Proven Ways To Increase Sales
Now! 121

Introduction.

This book serves as a monument to the superb individuals that I have had the honor of working with and learning from. They have contributed to shaping, molding and honing my selling skills into who I am today. At the relatively young age of 36, I have studied the masters over the last decade and a half and have accomplished more things than most people have never even thought possible.

When I first started selling almost 17 years ago, I thought that I would be better off in a different career. I was so bad; my mom would not even buy from me! I cut my teeth selling life insurance part time. Talk about a tough gig!

I bought into the misconception that in order to sell, you had to talk a mile a minute. I, of course, learned the real lesson of sales the hard way. I was not paid!

Over the last seventeen years or so, I have excelled in several different industries: insurance, import/export, auto accessories, advertising, magazine sales, wholesale, and automobiles among others. I have sold to businesses, consumers, and everything in between, even door-to-door! If you have never knocked on a cold door (homes or offices), you have no idea what tough is.

There is no fat or theory in this book. Everything within these pages is utilized from my real-life practical application. They are field tested and proven to work. I have used these ideas and strategies. Not only have I taught them to people that I have worked with, but also professionals that have worked for me. Moreover, I continue to teach them to my clients today from a wide variety of industries.

These techniques work regardless of what you sell or whom you sell to. All I ask is that you try them out. It would be a tragedy if you did not use the one thing that could have given you the greatest result in your selling career just because you "thought" it would not work!

Unlike some of the authors and trainers you may have come across, I continue to sell every single day. I am in the trenches, as a sales professional, just like you. I face the same challenges, the same obstacles and the same frustrations that you do. I know exactly what we, as sales professionals, go through on a daily basis.

In today's economy, being good is not good enough. With the way that buyers are more sophisticated and perceptive, you need to be great. You need to be great in two categories:

Skill Set and Mindset.

Skill sets are the tools of selling, asking for referrals, knowing what and how to say something during your presentation, dealing with objections, prospecting strategies, marketing systems, trial closes and everything in your sales tool belt. Skill set is the knowledge.

Mindset is having the attitude and fortitude to utilize our skill sets. It is having the focus and determination of continuing to use our skill sets even in the face of rejection, of possibly losing the sale, or making phone call after phone call. Mindset is applying the knowledge.

So which is more important? They both are! The key to developing mindset and skill set is constant exposure and practice. You have to be excellent at developing both of these areas.

Read this book not just once or even twice. Read it over and over again. One of my goals with this book is to give you constant exposure to the skills and strategies that have helped me over the years to become a success. I did not learn everything all at once; neither did I become proficient in everything all at once. It took time, and I added to my skill level one item at a time and improved in one area at a time. I would like you to use this book the same way.

You should read the whole book, implement the changes and practice the improvements one at a time. Keep on coming back to this book to refresh the information. I promise that each time you read it, you will learn something new, or you will remember something that you may have forgotten. I am going to provide you with the tools to develop not only highly advanced sales skill levels but also rock-solid mental fortitude.

I have identified key areas for anyone in a revenue-producing role. The strategies and techniques in this book are not theory. I learned them and applied them. Not everything will apply to you, and not everything will work 100% of the time. I do know that they work enough times for you to be successful at what you do. I would encourage you to keep an open mind and try out everything before saying *"this doesn't sound like it's going to work"*. I have personally used everything that I share in this book and <u>they do work</u>!

This book is organized in easy to read chapters. Each one of them will teach you specific skills and strategies that will help you to increase your production, thereby increasing your income. If you were able to do that, you would not be upset, would you?

So happy reading and Best in Success!

Chris Randolph

PART A:
SKILL SET

Chapter 1:
How People Make Buying Decisions

We human beings are very interesting animals. We are probably the only species on the planet with the ability to have an advanced intellectual thought process.

Think about this... People have the ability to reason, make decisions, change those decisions and proceed with a sense of purpose and direction. This is very apparent especially when we make buying decisions. In my workshops and with my coaching clients, I usually ask this question, "How do people make decisions?"

I get all kinds of responses. When you come right down to it, it usually boils down to two main reasons; emotional and logical. Actually, that is not entirely accurate.

There is generally only one reason. People, in general, more often than not, make pretty much all of their decisions based on emotion. They simply use logic to justify their emotional decisions.

People buy for their reasons and not yours.
*People buy for emotional reasons and then **they justify it with logic.***

Think about that last car that you bought. It made you feel good, it made you seem exciting, or it made you feel special or successful. When you buy something based on emotions, you are satisfying a want.

When I bought my first car, it was an Alfa Romeo 164. It was a beautiful red car. It was fast and had a powerful engine. It had a great sound system.

It went fast and it made me feel good. The price was great and I told myself that I could afford the payments. Logically it made sense. I will let you in on a little secret. If the payments were twice as much, I still would have gotten the car.

A few years ago, my wife and I were discussing purchasing a truck. The logic I was using on her was that "every household needs a truck", so we needed one too. She was somewhat open to it and so a few days later, I visited the dealership where I used to work and drove off in a brand new Toyota T-100 truck.

On the way home, it hit me that we had never really discussed the details of the truck. We never agreed that we were definitely going to buy a truck. We had not even really decided on which truck to get or what our budget was. For you men, you know that I was in big trouble at this point. My reasoning was that sometimes the man of the house just makes some of these decisions.

I arrived home in that brand new truck. Just before I walked through the front door, I was suddenly very nervous about buying the truck without my wife knowing about it. Nevertheless, I told myself, "You're the man of the house. What you say goes!" I then felt more confident and walked in.

I started the conversation by saying that we really ought to get a truck and I reminded her that her favorite color was blue. I listed all the logical reasons on why we should have a truck in the household. She was not buying the line. I was starting to get nervous again. I was not selling her on the idea. I was in trouble now. However, I am the man of the house and what I say goes!

So I flat out told her that I had made a "head-of-the-household" decision and there was a beautiful, brand-spanking new blue Toyota T-100 sitting in the driveway. Realizing my authority, my wife did not say a word....and despite my best efforts; she did not talk to me for the next four days!

I had made a huge mistake in my methodology of selling her on the truck. Instead of focusing on the logical reasons of why we should have the truck, I should have concentrated selling her on the emotional reasons of why we should have one. I should have paid more attention to how she would **_feel_** about our family getting a new truck.

If we are able to find the reason (or to create the reasons), that appeal to the emotions, we, as sales professionals have it made. Stephan Schiffman (author of more than 25 books and audio programs) tells me that our greatest competitor is not the other guy or the other company. Our greatest competition is the *status quo*, or their current situation. Sometimes the more difficult task is convincing the prospect to change their current situation.

After all, they have been operating that way for a while. Why should they change just for you? They are comfortable, right? They are in their comfort zone. People are hesitant to change, especially if they have been doing it for a while.

The most important thing to remember is that they will not change for your reasons, but they will change for their reasons. They will change not because logic dictates it; but rather how they will feel about the decision.

Think about this. Even though the logic says that they should change, how they feel about change prevents them from doing so. That is important, so I will say it again. How they feel about change prevents them from changing. Your sole role as sales professionals is to effect positive change. You effect positive change by identifying emotional and logical reasons for the change (or why they need to purchase your product or service).

You want to build your questions, your presentation, your collateral material, and your "closes" to get your prospect to FEEL the benefits of using your product or service. You want them to feel the emotions on becoming your client. Let us look at Maslow's Hierarchy of Needs, as developed by Abraham Maslow.

Maslow's hierarchy provides several layers of motivational influences. Elements that are more fundamental motivational influences must be satisfied before next level elements become motivators. As a rule, the more luxurious or prestigious a product is, the higher the level the need is on Maslow's Hierarchy.

Using this as a basis, and the level at which our product falls into; we can actually tailor the presentation to fit these needs.

For example, if you sold Porsche, you would focus more on the status and the enjoyment rather than selling the need for transportation. On the other hand, if you sold home alarm systems, you would focus more on the safety aspect and the peace of mind. Selling a home on "millionaire's row" would be different from selling a home in a less affluent part of town. Even selling at different times to a same prospect would make a difference.

Batteries can sometimes be expensive if you buy them at the wrong place. Have you ever had this experience where you needed batteries bad enough that you did not care how much you paid for them? I have. In addition, later on I realized that I could have bought a dozen for what I had paid for two of them at the gas station. Batteries at the gas station? They know something about people, don't they?

Let's get into Maslow's Hierarchy of Needs.

Biological and Physiological Needs
These are biological needs. They are the basic human need for air, food, water, and sleep. They are our strongest needs because if we were deprived of all needs, the physiological ones would come first.

Safety Needs

When our physiological needs are satisfied and are no longer controlling thoughts and behaviors, the needs for security will be the next priority. We generally have little awareness of security needs except in times of emergency or periods of disruption.

Love Needs and Sense of Belonging

When the need for safety and for physiological well-being is satisfied, the next class of needs is love, affection and "belongingness". We seek to overcome feelings of loneliness and alienation. We want to be accepted.

Needs for Esteem

When the first three levels of needs are satisfied, the pursuit for esteem can become dominant. These involve needs for both self-esteem and for the esteem that a person gets from others. We have the desire for a stable, firmly based, high level of self-respect, and respect from others. When these needs are met, we feel self-confident and valuable as a person in the world. When these needs are frustrated, we tend to feel inferior, weak, helpless and worthless.

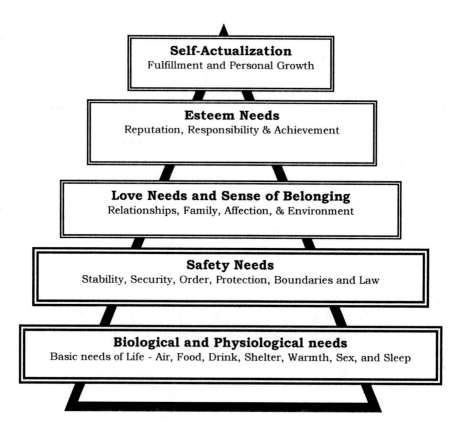

Needs for Self-Actualization
When all of the other needs have been fulfilled, then the need for self-actualization is activated. Maslow describes self-actualization as a person's need to be and do that which the person was "born to do".

Using Maslow's Hierarchy of Needs as a guide, it shows us how to position our product or service, depending on the need it fulfills. The simplest way to determine the need is to ask why they want it or how they would be using your product if they were to get it.

The bottom line is to sell to the customers' desires by finding out what motivates them.

What is a buyer fingerprint? It is the technique of determining the criteria that a prospect used in the past to make a buying decision for a similar product or service.

People are creatures of habit. They normally do the same things, shop at the same stores, eat at the same restaurants, buy the same kind of cars, wear similar style of clothes... well, you get the idea. We are creatures of habit.

It has been said that there is no "Magic Answer" in the profession of selling. And that is absolutely right. There is no substitute for hard work. However... if there were a "Magic Answer" in sales, it would be the strategy of "Buyer Fingerprints".

With this line of questioning, the outcome is to elicit information on how a prospect has made a similar decision on a similar product in the past.

It is as simple as asking,

"When you bought this car 3 years ago, what were some of the things that made you decide it was the right one?"

"How did you manage to decide that this home was the perfect home for you and your family six years ago?"

"If you were to decide to get this today, what are some of the things that you would have to consider?"

"What did you have to discuss with your wife in order to make that decision?"

So with all of this information, you will have a good idea on how your prospect is going to make their decision on whether they are going to buy or not. You must appeal to your prospect's emotions.

If you have no idea why people are buying from you, then you have a couple options. The first is that you can continue doing what you are doing. And there is nothing wrong with that if you are satisfied with your current results.

Alternatively, you could go to your clients, the people that have bought from you, and find out why they did. Find out what made them decide to buy from you. Find out how they felt about you and what factors were considered when they made the decision to buy from you. Is it a little bit of work? Yes, it is. It will pay off because you are adding to your arsenal of knowledge.

I ask this question at my workshops, "How many of you want to make more money this year, than you did last year? The usual response is that every hand goes up and they are nodding and saying "yeah!"

Albert Einstein said, "Insanity is doing the same thing over and over again expecting a different result".

If you are going to do what you have always done, you are going to get what you always got.

So, in essence, if you want better results, better income, you need to do something different in your activities.

Oftentimes, when a salesperson is experiencing dismal failure, and he is asked about it, the reply is invariably "they're not in the market right now" or "they don't seem to be interested right now".

I was conducting a training workshop at a dealership in Anaheim and the salespeople in the training were a sharp bunch! After the session, I was walking around and looking at the cars. One of the salespeople was walking by and I started chatting with him. He started telling me that sales training does not work. I was pretty shocked by this statement and asked him why? He told me that the customers had changed.

I said, "What do you mean?"

He said that customers were coming in and wasting his time because they were not buying from him. He said that if they did not want to buy from him, there was nothing that he could do.

Then he said something that floored me!

"I'm a great salesman. If they want to buy the car, I can sell it to them. I'm good when they want to buy."

Are you this guy? If you are, I have some advice for you. You have two options: Get better at selling or get out of selling. Get out of selling before you make a bad name for the rest of us.

How many times have you heard these phrases during a sales meeting? Or how many times have you uttered these words? I hope that you are not the one always saying these things.

"Being in the market" would be the equivalent of a car's fuel gauge showing "E" for empty and needing to buy gas. Or like the household that ran out of milk or sugar. These people are in the market now for gas, milk or sugar.

This is true for a need in our lives, usually for the necessities. We all buy these things without a sales pitch or presentation by a salesperson, don't we?

The thing is we do not just buy necessities, do we? We all buy things that we want or desire. The want or desire can come internally or from external factors, i.e. sales professionals.

Usually, the average salesperson relies on logical points or the "features" of the product or service. They talk about quality, price, durability, technological advancement, efficiency and "everybody's doing it".

While it is important for the sales professional to believe and understand these factors, by themselves, they are not going to influence the prospect. While they may be important, they may not appear to be important to the prospect.

A sales professional has to take the features and turn them into benefits. He needs to talk about them and demonstrate to the prospect that these are indeed benefits. The question to ask is, "What benefit or advantage will my customer get out of this feature?"

A sales professional will include logic and emotion in their presentation for success.

Chapter 2:
Building Trust and Rapport

Have you ever had a sale that you lost and did not really know the reason why? We have all had this experience, right? You thought you had all the facts and figures right, but for some reason, you and the prospect just did not seem to click.

You have also had clients that just seem to be like "putty" in your hands, and everything is clicking just right and you cannot seem to do any wrong. They just want to buy from you!

When it was not clicking, there was a "disconnect" between the two of you and for some reason, you could not establish some form of common ground. Chances are you lost the sale because you did not establish a sufficient level of trust and rapport with your prospect.

Remember this: **NO TRUST = NO SALE = NO MONEY**

Is it possible to establish instant trust and rapport? The answer is a resounding "YES"! A pioneer in this field taught these techniques to me. The genius I am talking about is Dr. Donald Moine, PhD (author of *"Unlimited Selling Power"* and *"Modern Persuasion Strategies"*).

Establishing trust and rapport is essential to building a working relationship with customers. Without it, problem solving, providing customer service and selling become frustrating and daunting uphill battles. It is your job to make them comfortable. It is not their job to make you comfortable.

You see, people notice positive things subconsciously and they notice negative things consciously. If you are dressed nicely, well groomed and pleasant, your prospect notices this subconsciously. However, if you are shabby, with mismatched clothes and unshaven, you will stick out like a sore thumb in their conscious minds!

There are two different levels of building a relationship; they are "common ground" and "rapport". Once again, "common ground" is more conscious and "rapport" is more subconscious. The average salesperson usually ONLY relies on finding the common ground with a prospect and does not develop that relationship any further. This level by itself and undeveloped demonstrates the more amateurish and shallow attitude.

In my office, there are a couple large framed movie posters of "Pearl Harbor" and "Blade". They are huge! Like most managers and owners, we get salespeople visiting us trying to sell us their products and services. It always irritates me when they try to develop common ground with me by saying they love those movies as well! That is a trait of an average salesperson, an amateur.

A true sales professional would ask <u>WHY</u> I have those pictures. If they had bothered to find out, I would have told them that the pictures actually belonged to my landlord. The only reason they are on my wall is because I got tired of having them lean against the wall in my hallway!

There is nothing wrong with starting out with common ground. As long as you take the relationship along the path towards the next advanced step. Common ground is more superficial. For example, "You like the LA Lakers, I like the Lakers", "You come from a small town, I come from a small town", "You like fishing, I like fishing".

Do not get me wrong. There is nothing wrong with saying these things. Just develop them a little further than just stating the obvious with no attempt to go on a deeper level.

Rapport allows you to be more in harmony with your prospect. It causes the both of you to be in harmony and it subconsciously communicates, "I'm like you, you're safe with me".

Once you have developed trust and rapport you actually have the hard part behind you and you are probably going to make a sale! For you see, it really does not matter how knowledgeable you are about your product or how skilled you might be at closing, unless you have earned your prospects confidence, you are not going to make the sale period.

The bottom line here is that people want to do business with salespeople that they relate to and that they feel understand their needs.   Obviously, the challenge and importance of developing trust and rapport will escalate in direct relationship to the price of your product or service.

1. Be mindful of body language and gestures.
Remember to keep these gestures positive. Unfold your arms, uncross your legs, show your palms and remember to smile. Nothing makes a person look better than a smile.

Develop awareness and be mindful of your prospect's body language. You have to be an effective listener who notices all aspects of communication and is aware of voice tone, facial expression, repetitive movements, and muscle tension. Watch for inconsistencies between your prospect's spoken word and their nonverbal communication.

Rely on the nonverbal as a much more accurate indicator of intent.   It is not what we say, but how we say it.   By understanding your prospect's body language, you will minimize perceived sales pressure and know when it is appropriate to close the sale.

2. Pacing and Leading.
"Matching and Mirroring" your prospect's body language gestures will psychologically cause them to identify with you. The power behind this principle is firmly grounded in the precept that people trust people that they believe are similar to them.

Matching and mirroring is an unconscious mimicry by which one person tells another that he is in agreement with their ideas and attitudes.

Likewise, studies have shown that when people disagree, they subconsciously mismatch their body language gestures. You want to be careful not to be too obvious when you are consciously matching someone because it might be perceived as manipulative if you do not do it naturally. An effective way to begin matching is to subtly nod your head in agreement when your prospect nods their head.

3. Make eye contact and listen with genuine interest.
You are certain to create an unfavorable impression if you give your prospect the idea that you are not fully present in the conversation.

Unfortunately, we are often busy game-planning our response instead of truly listening to what is being said. I suggest that you occasionally repeat verbatim what your prospect says especially their key words or phrases. Restating in your own words serves to clarify communication, but you deepen rapport when you use their words.

> *If I say it, they can doubt me.*
> *If they say it, it must be true!*

4. During your needs analysis interview, ask open-ended, clarifying questions with who, where, what, when and how.
Open-ended questions will require your prospect to give in-depth responses. Become an active listener. While it is important to educate your prospect about your product or service, as a general rule you should listen more than you talk.

Keep your attention focused on your prospect and avoid the temptation to interrupt and dominate the conversation. The quickest way to destroy trust and rapport is to interrupt another person while they are speaking. If you do interrupt, minimize the damage by apologizing and ask them to please continue.

5. Dress and act professionally.

While it may seem unfair, we are judged on our appearance. Research indicates that people form a lasting impression of us within the first five minutes. Be personable but not overly familiar. If appropriate, occasionally call your prospect by their first name. The sweetest sound to the human ear is the sound of our own name. But do not overdo it.

Salespeople are hired to do four things;

1.   Prospect

2.   Make Presentations

3.   Close

4.   Get Referrals

Most salespeople are pretty good at making presentations. And when they are done making the presentations, they hit another stumbling block in "asking for the order".

President Eisenhower once said that, "*Persuasion is the art of getting people to do what you want them to do, and to like it.*"

You need to be always thinking about how you can get people to want to do the things that you need them to do in order for you to attain your objectives.

Whenever you can show a person that, via persuasion, they can avoid a loss or to obtain a gain of some kind, you can influence them to take a particular action. The very best appeals are those where you offer an opportunity to gain and an opportunity to avoid loss at the same time.

With enough rapport, you can get just about anyone to do just about anything within reason. You build your rapport by being sincere. I am not suggesting deceit or manipulation in any way.

The key behind building the highest level of rapport is what resides within you. It takes work to accomplish this. It takes a lot of work. Then again, our income that is tied to that, isn't it?

A good way to build rapport is to be a good listener. People love talking about themselves. People are more interested in themselves than they interested in you. Allowing your prospects to talk to you about themselves will go a long way in building and developing that relationship.

It takes time and practice to be a good listener, especially if you have never really done it before. You have to start from inside of you. Make a decision to care more about your prospects. I promise you, it goes a long way in furthering your credibility.

A word of warning; the kiss of death is if you ever interrupt your prospect.

<u>Never, never ever</u> do this.

I sometimes make a joke during my workshops when I say that some salespeople look like ogres! This usually gets a chuckle. Another joke is that if you are not "drop-dead gorgeous", you must be really good at your job!

For those of us that do not look like we could ever make it on the cover of GQ magazine, there is still hope!

One of the easiest and most wonderful things anyone can do to improve how they look is to smile. I am not talking about the silly grin or the Joker's perpetual grin. I am talking about the sincere pleasure that a good smile conveys.

In almost 100% of the time that you smile at someone, they will smile back. There is something infectious about a smile.

I would like to demonstrate this to you right now. Let's try this out. I want you think about a situation which caused you to feel depressed or sad. It may have been the last time a "hot" prospect said no to you and shot you down. Think about that for a few seconds.

How do you feel now? Not very good, I bet.

Now I would like you to take a deep breath and sit up straight. Put your shoulders back and smile, a big smile. Smile as if you mean it. Any difference in how you feel?
You feel different, don't you?

The positive feeling you just experienced came on as a direct effect from that smile. When you meet your prospects, smile when you shake their hands. Smile when you talk to them. They have no choice but to smile back. When they do that, they feel just a little bit better. Won't you try smiling just a little more?

When you have built rapport with your prospect, and you care about their needs and concerns, the relationship has transcended to a higher level. You are no longer "selling" them. You are helping them to make an informed decision, in which the natural progression will lead them to buy from you.

Chapter 3:
Successful Prospecting

Prospecting is exactly like fishing. You have to look for the right pond with the right prospects in it. You do not catch a fish every single time you cast your rod, exactly like you do not make a sale with every single prospect. But the chances of you landing a fish increase each time you cast your rod, exactly like the chances of you making a sale increase each time you have a qualified prospect.

In prospecting, like fishing, you need certain tools and skills. Your tools in selling are the skill sets. Being proficient in your selling skills and not using them is like having your rod and not knowing where to cast it.

So the very first step is to identify where you are going to fish. Where are you going to cast your rod? Ask yourself this question; "Where do my customers come from?"

One of the most crucial components in successful selling is finding the right people to present your offer to. Sales professionals are hired to find customers. Before you turn them into clients, they are prospects. Before you turn them into prospects, they are suspects. Before you turn them into suspects, they are just names on a list or leads.

Average salespeople are constantly bragging that their presentation is great. The only thing holding them back from gargantuan success is locating the people to make their presentation to.

There are people everywhere. There is no shortage of people to talk to. You have to get yourself out there to meet them and qualify them for your product and service.

Let's say you made a commitment to yourself to find and talk to 5 new people a day. In addition, if you did that for 5 days, you would have talked to an extra 25 people a week.

Suppose you kept that up for the whole month, you would have 100 people that you would have talked to and have the opportunity to follow up with. Over the course of a year, you could turn that 1200 people into prospects.
Imagine if you were to follow up with these 1200 people, how many of them might possibly, eventually do business with you?

Our clients that use this strategy tell us that they eventually close anywhere from 4% to 18% of the total number of people that they meet and talk to over the course of a year. The ratio depends on your product, how well you qualified them initially and the quality of the follow up.

Let's run some numbers. If you were a real estate agent that puts an average of $6,000 per transaction into your pocket, assuming only a 2% closing ratio, that is 24 transactions. With an average $6,000 commission for each, that is a whopping commission of $144,000!

Many salespeople have a fear of prospecting. When people respond to us in a positive way, we feel good. When it is negative, we feel bad. It is this not wanting to feel bad that causes us to not want to prospect.

I would like to stress that it is normal and natural for our customers to be initially uninterested in what we have to share with them. People will tend to always say "NO" as an automatic knee-jerk instinctive initial reaction and it is your job to listen to what they are really saying and to get them to listen. Remember; rejection is not personal.

If we are in front of prospects, isn't that when we are working as sales professionals? Let's discuss some prospecting strategies shall we?

Prospecting Strategies

1. The Buyers' Cycle

2. Adoption Technique

3. Advanced/Upgrade Selling

4. Lead Swap

5. Service/Technical Department

6. Trade Shows

7. Networking

8. Referrals

One of the easiest techniques is to prospect people that have already purchased your product or service before. The concept is more structured than just waiting for them to show up or call you. How do you know when someone is ready to buy again?

It's called the Buyers' Cycle. Can anyone tell me what this is? Any guesses?

Okay, in real estate, for example, the average family buys a new home every 5 or 6 years. For cars, it is a little shorter, normally every 3 or 4 years. When you tap into the Buyers' Cycle, these are times when a consumer is getting ready to make another purchase or at least is thinking about making another purchase.

What if you were able to swoop in like Superman when the time was right? Would that make a difference in your income and production? What you have to do is determine what the average Buying Cycle is for your product.

Of course, you have to keep in constant contact with your clients. You cannot just pop out of the blue and say, "Isn't it time for you to buy again?" This is where professionalism in being sales professional lies. Keep in constant contact.

The next strategy I would like to share with you is the Adoption Technique.

Every company has turnover right? Especially in the sales department. When a salesperson leaves a company, what do they leave behind? Yes, they leave behind their prospects and clients.

Abandoned prospects and clients have the potential to be a lucrative goldmine. All you have to do is follow up and keep in contact with them.

The upgrade method allows you to contact your existing customer base and offer them an advanced model or an upgrade on their current model or level of service.

Use this technique when your company introduces a more advanced product or when a higher level of service is introduced. Just like with the "Buying Cycle" technique, you cannot just swoop in and ask for the business.

You have to keep in touch with your clients and make sure you are in constant contact with them. In essence, you have to continue to build and solidify your relationship between a buyer and a seller into a relationship with a client.

The next technique is the lead swap. This is how it works, you form a club. Yes, a club of sales professionals. The members of this club share leads with each other.

One thing you want to make sure of is that each of the sales professionals is in non-competing industries. However, these industries should complement each other, or more specifically, the prospect can be shared by non-competing sales professionals.

For example, a mortgage broker might include in their group, a realtor, home insurance agent, home alarm and security specialist and interior decorator.

Implement this strategy by having your lead group meet on a regular basis. Have an understanding that each time the group meets, they have to bring and share 2 leads for another member of the group. For this strategy to be effective there needs to be a commitment on everyone's part to fully participate and support the rest of the group.

If your company has a service or technical department, this can be a lucrative place to fish for prospects. Usually when there is a situation that requires repair, this department has the information first.

You could make an arrangement where if any of the technicians came across a suitable prospect for you, they'd let you know right away and also mention to the client that you're going to get in touch with them to discuss the other possibilities.

For certain industries, participating in trade shows or even street fairs can be a goldmine. The goal of being at one of these is not to sell. If a deal falls in your lap, do not let it go. But the main aim by having a booth is to collect as many leads as possible during this time.

Make your booth inviting for someone to walk up to. But do not just sit there and do nothing. Be proactive in getting people to drop their contact information with you. But you do not want everyone or just anybody to give you their information. You are going to want to at least put them through a quick qualification process to even justify your time in following up with them.

Make your booth look attractive and fun. This will be inviting for prospects to come by your booth instead of walking on the other side of the aisle.

I often visit trade shows and street fairs where I see a salesperson sitting at the back of their booth looking at people walking past them like a lost puppy dog! What is this? If you are not going to do a good job, go home! Get positive-minded, positive-looking people to cover the booths.

Another important and crucial step is to follow up with these people. The real work starts after the show is over. Do not let them slip through the cracks. You have put in too much time, effort and expense to let it just slip away.

The most successful sales professionals prospect everyday. If you stop doing it for even one day, your future results will reflect that.

- Do something everyday because everything counts.

- Every phone call you make counts.

- Every email counts.

- Every fax counts.

- Every referral counts.

- Every appointment counts.

- And it all starts with prospecting.

So get out there and start prospecting!

Chapter 4:
Sales Scripts

As sales professionals, the words that we use can make or break us. Selling is more than just talking. The days of the mile-a-minute salesman in the checkered suit are long, long gone.

Having the right words will go a long way in the selling game. You are a "wordsmith". Your choice of words carries the weight in your presentation.

The first rule is; do not wing it! The average salesperson thinks they need to be flexible and spontaneous. They do not want to be tied down or restricted to a canned presentation. That is exactly why they are average.

You must have a primary objective for every call. Ask yourself' "What do I want them to do as a result of my conversation and what do I want out of the phone call?"

Remember, people tend to believe their ideas a lot more than yours. If you were to prepare questions that were in line with your call objectives, can you see how the conversation would have a different result?

Ask yourself this question, "What do I need to ask them, instead of just talking, in order to persuade them to move on to the next step in the process?"

When prospecting, don't start the call with, "I was just calling in your area . . ." People want to feel like they are the only person you are calling . . . not just one of the many that you are calling from a list. You have to treat each contact as unique.

Two things happen during every call. Either you sell them on why you would benefit them, or they sell you on why they do not need it.

What are you supposed to say during your call? It depends on the purpose of your call, or the aim in picking that telephone up.

Are you qualifying a prospect?

Are you trying to set an appointment?

Are you trying to follow up?

Are you trying to close the sale?

Or are you trying to achieve a combination of all four?

The key to your script is the vehicle by which you communicate your message. The components of your script should include the following:

1.   Opening
2.   Information Gathering
3.   Presentation
4.   Trial Close
5.   Objection Handling
6.   Close.

How do you feel when you hear this?

"Hello, Mr. Smith, you would you like to save $5,000?"

"Hello, how would you like to get a 50% return on a $10,000 investment?"

Don't they turn you off? Of course they do. Try this instead...

"Good morning Joe, this is Chris with ABC Company in San Diego, how are you doing today? The reason I am calling is that my company is providing homeowners in the area with complimentary home inspections. Many of your neighbors have found these complimentary inspections very useful in helping them identify potential problems."

The above opening has achieved several outcomes. You have called the prospect by name. Wished him a good morning (or afternoon, or evening as the case may be) showing that you are different from everyone else that has called him with a simple hello. It identifies you and your company. It tells him the reason for the phone call. It also gives him a benefit right in the beginning so that you can move along to the information gathering and presentation.

In this portion of your call, you really do not want to be rattling off facts, figures or barreling along your presentation. Use plenty of open-ended questions, or questions designed to elicit a "Yes" response.

"You'd like to find out if there were any potential problems before they become too expensive to fix wouldn't you?"

"If there was no cost or obligation for the inspection, you'd want one of our highly trained inspectors take a look at your house or foundation, right?"

"What would you think the most important function is of a home inspection?"

These questions can also double as trial closes. You should consider trial closing right from the beginning of the phone call.

For example:
"Is Tuesday a good day for our inspector to come out?"
For the objections, it has been said that there are an average of 7 to 12 main objections in any industry. You need to list down all of these objections and write down responses to them.

Come up with at least 4 or 5 responses to each objection. You never know when you are going to need to use all of them. Do the same thing for all the closes that you use, that the top people in your office use and the top people in your industry use.

When you implement this, you will come to realize that your script is integral to your success. Do remember that just no two prospects are exactly alike. You need to be conversant enough with your script that you can be flexible and from which you can deviate as and when the situation warrants.

If you are like most salespeople, you have difficulties in picking up that 100lb phone. However, especially in today's changing economy, telephone communication is a remarkably powerful medium. A ringing phone is a powerful call to action. It is human nature to need to pick up a phone that is ringing.

The first thing I would like to ask you about cold calling is; "Are there any of you out there that absolutely love a cold call"? For those that answered no, do not worry! You are normal. For those that answered yes, my next question is what medication are you on... and can I have some of it!

One of the principles that I was taught is that anybody can make a sale. Actually, the specific words used were, "Even a blind squirrel finds an acorn once in a while".

Only a professional can have a sales career. Only sales professionals can make a career out of closing sales day after day after day.

One of the key things to remember is that if you take the necessary steps to project a positive image over the phone, it is relatively easy to accomplish that. On the flip side, if you have a negative attitude, then it is going to be very apparent to all that you talk to.

Many sales people are afraid of the phone. It is almost as if the telephone is a barrier to making a sale. Most salespeople think that for a sale to be closed (especially on big-ticket items); it has to be done in person. I have found that to not to be the case.

Since 1998, I have made over 185,000 cold calls (at the time of this writing, and still going strong!). Interestingly enough, countless products and services that you would never have guessed could possibly be sold over the phone have been and can be sold over the phone.

As a sales professional using the phone as your main method of communication, you perform a function that very few people in the world could do well, or would even want to try. And that is persuading someone to take action and make a decision, based almost solely on the words and ideas that come from your mouth. It is quite an awesome feat when you think about it. And do think about it. It takes a talented individual to be able to do that well. You have made a choice and you are that person.

Feel proud of what you do, and always strive to get better!

When we talk about professional telephone selling, I do not mean the poor schleps that call around dinnertime offering a lower mortgage rate or to switch your long distance service. Seriously, are we that hard up that we are banging our heads on the wall trying to save a penny a minute?

Professional salespeople should embrace the phone. If you do not use the telephone, you are wasting valuable time.

Imagine this: in a full 8-hour day, assuming you did not take lunch or any breaks, what is the maximum number of people you can see in person in a day?

Let's say it takes 30 – 45 minutes for an appointment. With just 15 minutes in travel time between appointments, we are talking about 8 people in a day that you can physically visit with. That is just about one prospect an hour.

Now some of you might be thinking that seeing 8 prospects a day is pretty darn good. Realistically, is that possible every single day?

Probably not.

Over the telephone, assuming 15 minutes is required for each "visit"; you can speak with 4 prospects an hour! This means 32 a day. Now, that is pretty darn good! Not to mention the savings in time, sweat, shoe leather, wear and tear on the car, parking, and gas.

Have you ever driven for half an hour or more for an appointment with a prospect? And for some unknown reason, he is not there or in a crucial meeting when you show up. Ever happen to you? ME TOO!

The telephone allows you to prospect, make presentations, and close the sale efficiently, effectively and professionally.

"Excellence has a structure. This structure can be duplicated"

What it simply means is if you do the things that successful people do; you will be successful too. There are ways to align yourself to the structure of excellence. This section is dedicated to sharing these structures of excellence that you can implement right now and achieve immediate results.

This section will not have all the answers. However, the basic skills will help anyone who sells by phone to project a higher level of credibility and professionalism. By using these strategies, you will have a competitive edge.

Tip #1:   Use The Right Tools

All professionals have their own set of tools that they use in their business. Mechanics have their wrenches, carpenters have their saws, dentists have their drills, architects have their draft boards and doctors have their stethoscopes. You, as a sales professional, have the tools of your trade that you need as well.

The first tool is of course the telephone. What is the big deal, you might ask; "I already have a phone". As a professional, ALWAYS use a headset. It keeps your hands free so you can jot notes, find files, type on your computer and of course, write up the order! You have several options; a trip to your local Radio Shack will be a good start.

If you want the best equipment you can get your hands on, consider Plantronics, in my opinion, the best value for performance out there. Headset telephones range from $10 all the way up to $400. Comfort is more important than price, especially if you are on the phone 8 hours a day. Try out several different models to see which one offers you the most comfort for your buck.

The next tool is a mirror. Get a mirror and hang it where you can see yourself when you are making your phone calls. Believe it or not, the person you are talking to can sense when you are not upbeat or feeling glum. Smile at yourself in the mirror. When you can see yourself in the mirror, you will be able to tell if you are smiling or not. I promise you, you will see a difference and your prospects will feel the difference too.

The next tool is paper and pen for "notepad listening". The intent behind this concept is that you should be making notes on your prospect. The most important thing you should write down is your prospects' name. Do this so that you do not forget the name, or call him by the wrong one. Nothing will hurt you more than calling your prospect by the wrong name.

You should also jot down what your prospect says, his likes, dislikes, and his "hot buttons". That way, you can focus all of your attention on your prospect. In addition, the notes that you make are a ready reference or reminder in case you need to refer to something that was mentioned earlier.

The next crucial tool that you need is your script. Before you get all twisted about using a script, understand that I am not talking about merely reading from a sheet of paper. You use your script as a guide. You must constantly practice your script so that it sounds natural, as if you are having a conversation.

Tip #2:   Lead/Prospect Organization
Have you ever had a "hot" lead and then could not find the business card or the piece of paper you wrote it on? Never did make the sale to that "hot" prospect, did you? You left money on the table didn't you? You cannot close them if you do not call them. You cannot call them if you cannot find their number.

You need to come up with a system where you can easily track your leads and prospects. Also, please do not confuse a lead with a prospect. A lead is a contact where you have not determined if they are suspects or prospects.

If you prefer a hands-on system, put everything on 3 x 5 index cards. Then use a tickler system. It's also sometimes called the "shoebox" system. Use your imagination according to how you want to re-contact your prospects.

When I use my system, if a prospect said to call next Tuesday, I would place that index card in next Tuesday's slot. If they said to call next month, I would place that index card in next month's slot. When next month rolled around, I would be ready to call them.

Needless to say, that anything mentioned or discussed should be notated on the index cards. Do not rely on your memory.

For the serious salesperson, consider using prospect management software like Microsoft Outlook, ACT! or Goldmine. I would recommend ACT! or Goldmine. These two programs are practically designed for sales professionals. With these programs, you can sort your leads and prospects; you can schedule appointments, meetings, activities and phone calls.

You can even set these up so that you are notified when its time to make that phone call. There is also space to place all kinds of information about your prospects, for example, birthdays, spouse's name, hobbies, interests, and so much more. If you are planning on staying in the sales profession longer than 30 days, you need a system for tracking.

Tip #3:   Ask For the Sale
Need I say more?

Tip #4:   Hire A Sales Coach
Coaching is not to be confused with consulting, psychotherapy, training, and teaching or mentoring. It is completely unique.

The primary role of a sales coach is not only to help sales professionals clarify their business and personal goals, or help craft an action plan that helps move them forward into action, but also holds them accountable each step of the way.

It is not a question of whether it will work, or if it is going to work. The fact is that it has been proven to work!

Experienced salespeople know that outstanding sales performance is the result of practicing the basics on a regular basis. A sales coach offers you the opportunity to reinforce, strengthen, create and maintain excellent sales habits, which will propel you to the top of your industry

A sales coach works with top performers to create outstanding results. Olympic athletes work with a coach to win the gold medal. Similarly, your sales coach will push, challenge, and demand more of you to break sales records, make more money, and bring your career to a new level.

The coach that you select should be extremely proficient in bringing out the skills and talents inherent in you. The coaching plan should be a multi-stage process that focuses on identifying and maximizing your strengths while increasing your awareness of your weaknesses and limitations. This is done so that these areas requiring improvement can be worked on.

I believe so strongly in the power of effective sales coaching that I am going to offer you a complimentary 45-minute coaching session. There is no cost for this session because I want you to experience the power of coaching first-hand. Because I am bearing this expense, you will be put through a quick qualification process.

For those of you smart enough to take advantage of this phenomenal offer send an email to info@thesalesedge.biz with "Coaching" in the subject line.

Chapter 5:
Referrals And Networking

Most salespeople will say that a referral is easier to close that a cold prospect. Why do you think that is? There is a level of rapport there because someone that they know and trust has referred them to you.

Yet, most salespeople do not ask for referrals. They do not ask because they are afraid to or they do not know how to ask. They are afraid because of the last 10 times they asked for a referral they only got one or even none.

Most salespeople usually say, "Here's my card, if you know of anyone that can use my product, please have them give me a call".

The very first thing you can do if you are not asking for referrals right now is to start asking. If you do not ask, you do not get. If you ask, you might just get it.

If you are already asking, good for you! We are going to fine tune what you are saying right now.

Ask yourself honestly how you rate as a sales professional in the area of referrals. This is the first step. Are you proficient at asking for referrals or do you suck at it? Either way, it does not really matter. What is important is that we get better, isn't it?

Develop a referral system.
A technique for removing the hesitation in asking for a referral is to tell your client or prospect that you are going to ask them for referrals. What's that? Yes, tell them you are going to ask for referrals.

"Mr. Prospect, I'm going to do a great job for you. When we are done, I am going to ask you if you agree that I did a great job.

And if you say I did a great job, I'm going to ask you for referrals, is that fair?"

How can your prospect say NO to that?

So when either the job is done, or almost complete, you can say "Mr. Prospect, remember I had mentioned that I was going to ask you if I did a good job? Well, did I?"

They will say yes if you did.

Then say, "Well, I'm glad you feel that way. We had also agreed that when I did a great job for you, I would ask for referrals".

And that is how you make it easy to ask.

I learned how to ask for referrals through trial and error and with a ton of input from Bob Burg, the author of *"Endless Referrals"*.

Utilizing Bob's powerful techniques, I have developed what I need to say. In my business, we depend on referrals. This is what I say:

"I'm growing my business in Southern California. As you know, I work heavily with referrals. A good referral for me is a business owner, sales manager or network-marketing leader with 6 or more people on their team that wants to increase their production. Think about companies that you have worked for in the past, companies that you do business with or would like to do business with. Out of all the people you know, can you think of anyone that fits this description?"

There are several components in the way that I ask for referrals. In fact, the first thing I do is I let my prospects know that I am going to ask them for referrals. I tell them I am going to do a great job for them. When we are done with the transaction, if they agree that I have done a great job, I will be asking them for referrals.

Therefore, this sets the stage. When we are done with the transaction, I ask them if I did a great job for them. More often than not, they answer yes. So I then remind them that I had told them that if I did a great job, I would ask them for referrals. This gives you the "authority" to get referrals from them because they had already agreed in the past. Can you see how simple this is?

The first component in asking for the referral is that you give a reason. In my case, the reason is that I am growing my business in Southern California and that I rely heavily on referrals.

The next thing that I do is educate them on what a good referral is for me. In my case, a good referral is a manager or business owner with 6 or more salespeople that want to or need to increase their production an income.

I then jog their memory by mentioning a couple things like places they have worked at before, companies that they currently do business with or even companies that they would like to do business with.

You can also offer an incentive to you prospects and clients for referrals. They could range from having lunch on you to cash incentives. It is up to you and what you feel is appropriate for you and your company.

People are generally lazy. Not everyone, but most are. It is easier to say no than to have to crack you brain to give you a referral. So you can do a couple things to make it simple.

We have what we call a "referral form" with the referral request printed at the top of the sheet. Then there are spaces for them to write in the referrals with some information that we will need, like their name, the company they are with and contact numbers.

Another thing we will do is ask them for access to their rolodex, PDA, contact management software, telephone and address book and go through it with them.

It has been said that everyone knows at least 250 people on some level. Is it really that hard to get at least 5 referrals out of each of our clients and prospects? It really depends on how badly you want it.

Let's run some numbers. If you managed to get 3 referrals from every prospect and client that you meet on a daily basis, with the assumption that you only have 3 of those a week. In one week, you would have collected 9 referrals. For the moment, let's forget about those referrals giving you referrals. In one month, you would have 36 referrals. In one year that would jump dramatically to 932 referrals! Isn't that something!

Can you imagine how your business would grow if you made a commitment to ask for referrals at every contact?
Let's take it a step further in our analysis.

I would like to run some of your own numbers. First, ask yourself these questions: What is the value of a good referral?

What do you get out of a referral?

What is the average commission in your business nowadays, not high, not low, just average? Remember how all salespeople agree that it is easier to do business with a referral than it is with a cold call? So with referrals, you save time and effort to make your commission, right?

If you follow these suggestions, you will never feel like you are bothering a prospect or a client ever again. You will not feel that getting referrals is hard or impossible. If you follow your referral system, you will not mess up the sales or the conclusion of the order.

In fact, one of the first things you can do right now is call your best clients and ask them for referrals. Imagine if you were to get one referral out of every one of your best clients. What would the potential income be for you?

Do not delay. Schedule these calls in your planner now.

In a networking environment, you usually have a whole bunch of salespeople trying to sell to each other. Almost everyone simply cares about themselves or their outcomes. Or even worse, they go with a colleague and spent most of the time chatting with their co-worker instead of meeting the other participants.

In these gatherings, make yourself stand out from the crowd. Instead of focusing on yourself and what you want, remember one of the concepts of building rapport is finding out what the other person wants and helping them achieve their outcome.

When you introduce yourself to someone, find out what they do and get their business card. Look it over with interest (and not a fake interest, please). Then ask them to tell you exactly what they do and what benefit they bring to a prospective client. Then ask them what a good referral is for them. Do you think you might just grab their attention? Of course you will!

When they describe what a good referral is for them, make sure you write it down. Then let them know that if you come across anyone that fits their description, you will definitely get in touch with them.

The next day, send a short note to all the people that you met reiterating what you had spoken to them about. This will leave a lasting impression on them. Keep in contact with them and of course if you come across a good prospect for them, let them know.

The key behind this strategy is that you are going to create advocates that will remember you because you went out of your way to find out about them and their business. You demonstrated a sincere desire in wanting to get to know them and what they do. You may or may not reap immediate dividends through this technique, but you will definitely build high-quality relationships.

A very important point to remember is that you are in this for the long haul. There is no "quick fix", especially in creating advocates to help you in your business. In this day and age of instant gratification, creating all of this and nurturing it takes time and consistent action.

Imagine that you are a farmer. Even before you plant your seeds for your crop, you have to prepare the soil, service your equipment and conduct a lot of preparation. Then, and only then, do you plant your seeds.

When this is done, you have to nurture your field with care, fertilizer, pesticides, water and nutrients. After several months of hard work, you harvest your crop. Payday!

You, as a sales professional, are exactly like a farmer. Nurture your business. And just like the farmer, nurture different "fields" of prospects that yield different crops at different times.

Do not just rely on one avenue of business. Conduct a variety of prospecting activities. Sometimes different methods of prospecting yield different results at different times. To make sure your business and production is consistent, use different methods of prospecting. Prospecting is the lifeblood of your business.

Chapter 6:
Power Negotiating Secrets

What is negotiation?

Is negotiating "bargaining", "shopping around", "talking about price, terms & conditions in a business deal"? I believe it is all of these things and more. It is almost a way of life. I believe negotiation and some form of it has been around since man was born.

Now, I never realized this before, but I have been negotiating since I could talk. And I will share something with you: So have you!

If you have kids like I do, you know exactly what I am talking about. Tell me if this sounds familiar.

"Dad, can I have $40 bucks to go for a movie with my friend?"

"What! $40! You don't need $40 for that"

"Okay, Dad. Can I get $30?"

"I'll give you $20 and I want you back by 9"

"Okay Dad!"

Sounds familiar, doesn't it? Of course it does. It happens everyday.

Dad may have been willing to give up to $30 and have his son home by 10pm. So Dad came out ahead in both areas. However, the son was willing to be home by 8 o'clock and get $20. So who really won? Well, they both did! They both won.

Both of them walked away from the negotiation session feeling happy and satisfied. That is what we would like to see in every situation, don't we?

We all want and desire many things in our life; money, recognition, freedom, love, affection, acknowledgements and security. There are some of us that know how to get more of these things and some that will get less. What is the difference?

The difference is in knowing how to negotiate effectively. After implementing the strategies in this chapter, you will know how to negotiate effectively.

Someone once said, "It's not what you know, or who you know, it's whether you know how to negotiate effectively".

This is certainly true, isn't it?

In negotiations, even though there is perceived conflict or differences in outcomes, both parties generally have or need a dependence on each other.

About twelve years ago, I started studying the topic of negotiating and made a decision to master it. Implementing these strategies over the last decade or so, testing them out and gauging their effectiveness and ease of use, I have negotiated business deals with companies from countries as far away as China and Russia.

I have negotiated in several hundreds of different situations and have learned from each of them. In this chapter, I will share strategies; tactics and tips that will help you become a better negotiator. Please understand that not every strategy will work every single time. They will work enough times to give you that edge. They key to using them effectively is using them!

First, let us talk about the possible outcomes of any negotiation situation. There are only 4 possible outcomes. Let's see what they are.

I Lose - U Lose

I Win - U Lose

I Lose - U Win

I Win - U Win

These 4 outcomes are the only possible results. Let's briefly go through each one. I am going to use the same circumstances in each scenario. Let's say I am trying to buy a brand new car.

In the "I Lose-U Lose" scenario, it could be where I do not purchase the car that I want and the salesman and the dealership does not sell the car. I lose out by not getting the car that I want, and the dealership does not get to sell a car.

In the "I Win-U Lose", I get the car, but at a price, that hurts the salesman or dealership.

In the "I Lose -U Win" situation, I get the car, but at such a high price that is way over retail and the salesman and dealership make a killing off the deal.

With the final scenario, the "I Win-U Win", all parties walk away from the situation happy. In successful negotiations, everybody wins.

Which outcome would you like to be in, when you negotiate? Yes, the WIN-WIN of course.

Now that we understand what negotiation is, the several different outcomes of any negotiation session, I would like to briefly share a concept called negotiation judo.

Why is a master a master? It could be any discipline, whether martial arts, education, sculpting, business, or whatever the case may be. You must practice and use the skills all the time, every single time. As a negotiation master, you need to be familiar with all of the strategies on this program and be able to use them in any given situation.

This brings us to the next area of discussion: Preparing For Negotiations.

Preparation is absolutely necessary in all areas of business. It is no different in a negotiation environment. The absolute first thing you have to do is determine your outcomes.

Let's say you are going into a situation that you know will entail face-to-face negotiations with your opponents. How would you prepare for such a situation? Can you predict the strategy of the opposite camp?

There is only one answer. Preparation! You have to know what you want and what the other party wants. You should list out your expectations. What you absolutely must have, what you would like to have and what you are willing to give up. Then you should list out the opposing party's expectations. What they absolutely must have, what they would like to have and what they would be willing to give up.

Discovering your objectives might not be that hard. Finding out about the other party's objectives is a little harder isn't it? How can you find out? You ask them! Or you ask others that know them.

In simple negotiations, you probably don't need to conduct extensive research, but every little bit counts, doesn't it?

I will give you an example, the difference between first and second place in the 100-meter sprint is more than likely less than one hundredths of a second. The amount of time is miniscule. Nevertheless, the rewards are certainly different, aren't they?

How can we get the edge in negotiating? Right now, we are going to go into negotiation techniques, tactics and strategies. I am going to cover several effective ways to gain the upper hand.

First technique I would like to share with you is called "Can you do better than that?"

Some time ago, I had to tile the floor in my family room, dining room and kitchen. Now my wife is a better negotiator with me than I am with her. She gets me to do all kinds of stuff that I do not want to do all the time. Some of you know exactly what I am talking about.

Anyway, this was not a project that I wanted to undertake on my own. It was about 800 square feet of tile work. So I proposed to her that we hire a tile guy to do all the work. Being the master negotiator that I am, she agreed with me!

The first thing I did was contact several tile guys to get them to come out, take a look and price out the job. This was the first round. After a couple days, I received several quotations by fax. I picked out a couple of them and started my negotiations with them. It was very interesting to say the least. How the contractor that finally got the job is the story, I will share with you.

His quote came in at $4200 for the job. I got him on the phone and we started talking about the job. He answered all of my questions. I was satisfied with his level of expertise and confidence in the project. Then we started talking about the price.

I said to him,"$4200 is a pretty good price, can you do better than that?"

He says," Let me think for a minute". He's quiet for a while and then he says," I can do it for $3500"

I then said, "That's great! Can you do better than that?"

He then says, "I can drop it down to $3300"

What do you think I said next?

That's right! "Can you do better than that?"

His answer was, "I can't drop the price any lower. But I can provide you with the thin set and the grout. You're going to need 25 bags of thin set and 5 bags of grout."

Now, I had been pricing the tile, thin set, grout and other materials in preparation for the project. Thin set was about $15 per bag and grout was about $6 a bag. By my calculations, it would come up to about $430. I was going to have to purchase the materials and would have had to spend the money anyway.

The tile guy giving me these materials and that meant I was saving money. The materials cost would have been $450 for the thin set and the grout and $2200 for the tiles for a total of $2650. Now because of a 5 to 8 minute conversation, the material cost had dropped by $430 and the labor cost had dropped by $900. A total savings of $1350!

I had saved $1350 by asking "Can you do better than that?"

Use this technique in any kind of negotiating situation. If someone is giving you a lower price, ask them if they can do better than that. You see the mind is like a question answering machine. Any question you ask the human mind, whether it is verbalized or not is automatically answered.

When you ask someone this question, their mind is automatically searching for the answer. They are asking themselves, "Can I do better than that?" If the answer is yes, they will. If the answer is no, they will tell you no.

This technique is so simple, effective and soft that no one can resist it. Try it out. That is the only way that you will know that it definitely works!

The next technique I would like to share with you is called the "flinch".

The flinch is exactly what it sounds like. You scrunch up your shoulders and wrinkle up your face as if you are in great pain. You can even add sound effects in like "Oooh" or grunting like it hurts or even gritting your teeth and sucking in air through it.

This is non-verbal communication in its simplest rawest form. It can be used to signal reluctance. This technique can be used with a low price, or a demand for a concession that does not excite you. The key is to act very natural and not like you are acting the feeling. Like with all of the techniques I am sharing with you today, you must practice.

Let me share a true-life example: I was looking for a family van and had purchased a pre-owned Toyota Previa van several years ago. At the place I was looking and considering buying from, the salesman had told me that the price of the vehicle was going to be $13500.

Upon hearing the asking price, I scrunched up my shoulders, wrinkled my face up and said "Aaaahh". I flinched.

His immediate response was, "I think I can get my manager to knock off $1500, what do you think about that?"

My response was," That's it?"

He replied "Well I think he'll drop the price lower than that, but I don't want to make any promises"

The responses I got were a direct result of the flinch. I did not even really have to say anything. I ended up purchasing the van for $11200. Not a bad deal at all.

Practice the flinch. It will save you money and more.

The next technique I would like to share with you is called the "Time Investment Strategy". This works extremely well in any situation, especially when you are the buyer.

The "Time Investment Strategy" utilizes the principle of the other party investing their time and effort in the process. When using this strategy, you want to make sure that the time and effort factor costs the other party a higher value than it costs you.

I will use the example of when I purchased the Toyota van that I had mentioned earlier. I first found out about the vehicle in an auto magazine called the Auto Trader. I called the dealership up and spoke to the salesman. I forget his name, so I will just use Jim in this story. I spoke with Jim a couple times over the phone clarifying some details on the van before I made that trip into the dealership.

When I got in, Jim spent about forty minutes showing me the van I was interested in. He was showing me the features on the vehicle and how I was going to benefit by owning it. Then we spent another 30 to 40 minutes looking at a couple other vehicles. By this time, Jim had invested almost an hour and a half of his time and effort.

Since this was around lunchtime, I told him I had to go back to work and said that I would come back later that evening. I also mentioned that before I made up my mind, I had to check with my wife. He was a little disappointed and it showed, but he had no choice, so he agreed.

I arrived at the dealership again that evening as promised. I went for another test drive with Jim. Half an hour later, we had the conversation I shared with you earlier. I had started that conversation with, "I'm really interested in buying that van".

Jim was probably thinking, "I certainly hope so after spending all that time with you!"

You see, Jim was in this for the long haul. He had spent over 2 hours with me at this point. When the time came for the proper negotiating, his position was weaker. He had traded his time in the hope of making a sale. His reward was contingent on selling me a vehicle. He wanted to sell me the vehicle. He needed to sell me the vehicle in order to justify his time that he had spent on me. He needed a return on his investment.

The negotiations went pretty well for me since my position was stronger. There were a couple times during the negotiations that I started to stand up and say I was leaving. The negotiations were concluded in my favor. I had set this whole thing up in such a way that acceptance of my terms were virtually guaranteed.

The next tip I would like to share with you is called Clarifying the Position Strategy. A friend of mine owns a business efficiency-consulting firm. When he was starting out, he managed to get himself in front of the final decision makers of a fortune 500 company. His presentation went very well. He was hitting all of their key points and it looked like he was going to get the contract.

At the end of the presentation, after they had talked about their investment of the contract, the CEO asked my friend a question, "How big is your company?"

This made my friend freeze. Since he was starting out with his partner, there were only two of them. He answered by going into a 10-minute explanation of all the affiliate offices they had in several states and a description of the other contracts that they had secured with other large companies. Without coming straight out and saying it, he was giving them the impression that the company was larger than it really was.

The CEO said, "That's too bad. We were hoping for a small hungry company. We want to be the largest client for the firm that we pick because we want to be the most important client of that company so the service would be at the highest level. We had one of the largest firms as our consulting company, the service was terrible, and we did not want to make the same mistake again. So we can't use your company."

That was too bad for my friend. What can we learn from this unfortunate episode?

Well, before you give an answer, clarify the question. In this case, "how big is your company" really meant, "what kind of service or what levels of service can you provide?"

One of the key rules in any negotiation situation is to clarify the other side's position. Do not make any guesses or assumptions.

Ask questions like, "What do you mean by that?" or "Can you tell me what situation happened in the past for you to ask this question?"

The next technique we are going to talk about is having the other party tell you what their price point is. You have probably heard in sales that the first person loses. While no one really loses in a win-win situation, it is possible to win less.

The general rule is that if you are buying, you want to buy as low as possible. If you are selling, you want to sell as high as possible.

Using this guide, because you are a better negotiator, you want the other side to tell you their figure first. Who knows, their figure may just be way higher than you expect.

A few good ways to elicit the answer is, "If we were to move forward on this, what is the price point you were hoping to get?"

Or "In a situation like this, what are you accustomed to receiving?"

Or something as simple as, "What kind of price range were you thinking of?"

Whatever answer you get, you can respond with the "flinch" or "can you do better than that?" or another variation which goes, "Is there any flexibility there?"

On the flip side, if you were to reveal your price first, you may have revealed a price lower than they had expected the negotiations to either start out at or that they had budgeted for this.
For example, a few years ago, I was trying to sell my laptop computer that was about three years old at the time. An associate of mine wanted to purchase it. He asked how much he could have it for and I told him I was not really sure. I then asked him what price he thought it out to fetch.

Now, before I move on, I should mention that I would have accepted $250. But did I tell him that? Of course not!

He told me he would pay around $350. I asked him, you guessed it, "Can you do better than that?"

After going back and forth, we finally ended at $465. If I had revealed my $250 figure, I would have collected less than that.

So never give out your figure first.

If you are not able to avoid this, there is a strategy to counter this. Always ask for more than you ever hope to get if you are selling. And if you were buying, always as for way, way less than you would ever hope to buy it for.

The next strategy is called "nibbling". It is used at the end of the major negotiation part of the process. You may or may not be familiar with the term, but once I have illustrated it with an example, you will definitely recognize it.

Let's say you enter a men's suit store intending to purchase a suit. You spend an hour or so with the salesman and he takes measurements of your neck, arms, shoulders and the rest of the areas that need measuring to pick out the right size.

You're asking questions about style, cut, and length and color coordination. After trying on 10 to 2 suits, you finally pick two or three suits that you like. You put the suits on one at a time to get them measured for the alterations. While that is happening, you innocently say," You're going to throw the shirts and ties that go with this suit, right?"

Everyone freezes. They don't know what to say. They have invested their time and effort. What goes through their head is if I do not give him at least the tie, he might not buy the suits. Next thing you know, I hear, "I can give you matching ties but not the shirts".

And that, ladies and gentlemen is the nibble. It is a simple effective method for asking for a concession as negotiations draw to a close.

Good salespeople are familiar with the power of knowing when to shut up. Is that important?

Of course it is. You do not want to talk yourself out of a deal do you? I used to work with a guy that just did not know when to stop talking. I would ask a closing question, shut up and wait for the other party to answer, and he would answer for them on his behalf! He would answer for them. Buddy, whose side are you on?

The basic rule is when you have asked a question, let them answer.

Another technique could be called the "Ultimatum" and a variation of that is the "Bluff". I am not going to spend too much time on this technique. I just wanted you to be aware of it. I would hesitate recommending the usage of this technique. Too many things have to fall into place for this to be pulled off.

Moreover, you do not want the other side to call your bluff and you are not going to be able or willing to back it up because of the investment of time, money or effort.

This technique works this way: If you do not do this or give me this, I will do that. In a simple example, you go to your boss and you tell him, "If you don't give me a raise right now, I'm going to quit and go join the competition!"

Your boss then tells you that you cannot have a raise. Since you gave your ultimatum, you either have to quit or stay in a weakened position. You bluffed, were called on it and the alternatives are not that attractive.

You can do a couple things to increase the chances of you succeeding in your ultimatum. With your ultimatum, you can use something that you know that the other party finds highly valuable or indispensable. We will breeze through the next couple of techniques because they are really simple.

The first of these is called reciprocity. Reciprocity means giving something to create a feeling of obligation. For example, when you begin negotiations, you present the other party with a welcome gift, or it could be something simple like paying for lunch.

When you give something to someone, they subconsciously become indebted to you. It is an unspoken exchange. They key is not to make a big deal of it, and not even bring it up at ay time in the future. If either of these things happens, it negates the gesture and it is a waste.

I have leather journals that cost me less than $20 each when I purchase them in bulk. They look elegant, they look expensive and they look very classy. I always have 5 or 6 of them with me at all times. I have softened people up with these leather journals when their heart was made of ice in the past. Think of something inexpensive that you can give away in this manner.

The next strategy is the giving up or granting of concessions. The idea behind this is to break through a stalemate, or to tip the other party over to close the deal. The concession can be very small or very large. It can be of extreme importance to the other party or not.

It works this way. Let's say the other party is asking for something extra over and above what you are all negotiating. You can choose to give in exchange for something that you want that they did not want to give up. Here is the syntax for this situation.

"I understand that you want the extra widgets. I will do that if you can find some way to give me the opportunity to speak with the other departments in your company to do the same thing for them, fair enough?"

That is how this works. You get a commitment for an exchange of concessions.

The next tip is using empathy. Not pity, but empathy. You lay your cards on the table and ask for their help. I was negotiating with a luxury car dealership on a training contract.

I told them that the reason we wanted the contract was that it would allow my company to break into the training the luxury car market and asked for their help as a reference in the future when we demonstrated that we did a good job.

The final tip I have for you is to take the extreme emotions out of your negotiations. What I mean by that is that there should not be any crying, tearing your hair out, emotional outbursts or tantrums of anger.

As a professional, there really should not be any extreme emotional outbursts on your part. This way you separate the people from the problem and you focus on the items of focus and not on individual positions.

If you choose to implement these strategies, you will be more successful in your negotiations.

Chapter 7:
How To Handle Any Objection

I believe the days of "old school" selling are over. Personally, I am tired of the out-dated concepts that were popularized by sales trainers subscribing to these methods. Would you believe there are still guys out there who still spout these tired and dated techniques like the Ben Franklin close or the *"press hard when you sign, its cheap carbon"*? If you do not know what that is, do not worry about it, you are not missing anything.

Nowadays, the prospects are about as well trained as we are and know their stuff inside and out. Excellence in selling is no longer the customer says this; you say that. Or the customer says that, so you say this. I am not talking about throwing scripts out the window or not learning the right words to say. I am talking about how sophisticated our prospects are becoming. In today's environment, being a success at selling is more like a chess game; it is a thinking man's game.

The days of the fast-talking, answer-for-every-question huckster are over. Today's greatest sales professionals listen more than they talk. The "sales rule" of listening to the prospect and presenting an idea that makes sense is almost what they have come to expect. Does this mean that we should not know how to handle objections or prepare responses to the objections that we get? Of course not.

Knowing all the objections that you get in your field and preparing the best responses to them will assist you in having more professional, convincing and more productive conversations with prospects.

We are all unique and have different ideas and different sales styles. You should have several powerful ways of handling each objection you are likely to encounter; if you do this, you will be far ahead of your competition.

Become familiar with the different ways of handling the objections. Speak your words with great feeling and sincerity. Do not say anything that you do not believe in 100%. It is not just the words, but also how we say them.

Our level of conviction determines whether what we are delivering sounds like a line or if we really believe in it ourselves. I would urge you to do some intense soul-searching regarding this area.

Review them constantly in order to maintain familiarity.

You, as a sales professional, must remember that objections are welcome in the sales process. Most of the time, the objection is merely a smokescreen for another underlying thought or hesitation. Your primary role is to handle the objection in an intelligent and professional manner in order to sweep it to the side and find out why they are saying what they are saying.

Do not be afraid when an objection pops up. It is the prospects' way of saying, "I need more information", or "There's something else on my mind, but I don't want to tell you what it is and I'll just say this instead."

Consider this; your role is to uncover the actual needs and desires of your client. Sometimes they do not know exactly what they want. They do not know exactly what they need. They do not know what the best plan or program is for them. That is your role. That is your responsibility. You are the professional.

Objections can be largely avoided by taking the right steps and doing everything correctly. When they do occur, resist the tendency to attack in defense. You must back up and revisit the questioning stage of the call. The voiced objection is quite simply, a symptom of the real problem, which you must uncover.

Most price objections start in the mind of the salesperson. Many sales reps are not 100% sold on the value of their product, therefore they are apt to offer price concessions even when the prospect does not flat-out ask, or they present price with a shaky tone of voice. Ask the right questions, present the results of what your product or service can do, and state the price boldly.

There are several ways of handling objections that you come across.

1.   Repeat the objection

2.   Clarify objection

3.   Answer by laughing

4.   Isolate the objection

5.   Answer with a question

6.   Answer with a story

7.   Ignore the objection

8.   Come back to it later

I am going to give you examples of each method using a specific scenario.

Examples:

1.   The fees are too high?

2.   What do you mean by the fees are too high?

3.   Other than the fees being too high, is there anything else holding you back?

4.   Why do you feel that way?

5.   One of my clients had said that to me and when he found out that the interest rate had been dramatically

dropped to 4%, and he was saving over $200 a month, he said," What the heck" and went with it.

6.   I understand. Let me tell you about the lower interest rate and the money you are saving ever month.

7.   I understand. Let me go over that after we have talked about the lower interest rate and how much you are saving every month.

Do we get objections in our line of work? Yes, everyday. Are objections reasons or excuses? Aren't they both? Salespeople think they are excuses and prospects think they are reasons.

Now, let me ask this, does anyone know the difference between an objection and a condition? A condition is a situation that exists that does not allow the prospect to use your product or service. It is a situation that prevents the prospect from buying.

How do we get away from talking to people with conditions? We qualify our prospects! There is a rule of thumb in sales:

1/3 of the people we talk to will buy from us no matter what we say or do.

1/3 of them will never buy from us no matter what we say or do.

That middle 1/3 is up for grabs <u>depending</u> on what we say or do.

Would you agree that in your industry you get the same objections over and over again everyday? They are always the same aren't they?

o   I'm not interested

o   I have to check with my wife/husband

o   Don't have the time

o   The price is too high

And so on.

Would it make sense to list out all the possible objections you get in your industry? Then brainstorm several responses to each objection. Do you each have ways of responding to objections? You way may be different from yours. You only know what you know. If you get together and brainstorm everyone's way, then you will know what he knows and he will know what you will know. You will have more tools in your tool belt.

Why people raise objections

They do not have enough information to make a decision

- They are afraid to make a commitment or decision

- They do not see a need or value in your product or service

- They do not want to buy from you or your company because they are not comfortable

- They need a little more time

- They need to get permission from someone else

3. Structure For Objection Handling

   i.   Hear it out

   ii.   Repeat it back

   iii.   Clarify it

   iv.   Isolate it

   v.   Answer the objection

   vi.   Confirm

   vii.   Move on (change the pace/trial close/close)

4. Methods of "Answering".

       a.   Solve the problem

       b.   Turn the objection into a benefit

       c.   Ask a question

       d.   Ignore it

       e.   Defer

       f.   Tell a story

       g.   Chuckle/Laugh/Ridicule

       h.   Guarantee

       i.   Facts & Figures

We will go through each one rather quickly.

a.   "I understand that the investment might be a little high to just write a check for it all at once. Would it help you out at all if we were able to break that up into 2 or 3 payments?"

b.   "I want you to understand that this automobile is one of the most luxurious around. Because of that, only the most successful and influential individuals can afford it"

c.   "How long has that been the case?"

d.   Just ignore it as if they did not even bring it up.

e.   "I'll answer that in a minute, I wanted to go over this part first, is that okay?"

f.   "Joe Smith over at ABC had the same concerns as what you had just mentioned. But because of our guarantee, he gave us the opportunity to service his account, and he's been happy since he got the service."

g.   "Ha! You are joking right? You can't be serious"

h.   "That's exactly why we have our rock-solid 100% money back guarantee. If anything ever happens, you'll get all of your money back."

i.   "If you notice here, this model produces 18.6% more horsepower than anything else out there, and is 24% less than our nearest competitor"

Another technique that you could use is a variation of the "Feel, Felt, Found" method. It is practically world famous because everyone has either used it or they have heard it used on them.

I would suggest keeping the structure of the "feel, felt, found", but giving it a modern twist. This is how the original works:

"I know what you're feeling. When I first saw it myself, I felt the exact same way until I found that our 100% guarantee covered every single component of this model."

My suggestion would be:

"You know, I hear what you're saying. That is very understandable. That had crossed my mind as well until I was informed (or I discovered) the 100% money back guarantee covered every single component of this model."

In your next sales meeting, make a suggestion that you brainstorm the objections that you get and list them out. When you have listed all of these objections you get on a daily basis, brainstorm the possible responses to them.

The next stage is to practice them and get better in your objection handling skills.

Chapter 8:
Asking The Right Questions

What is the easiest way to find out what a person wants? You ask them. A great mentor taught me this when I was a pup in selling: "If you don't ask, you won't get it. If you ask, you might just get it".

Get information before you give it. How could you ever make an effective presentation otherwise?

Always know where you will go with answers. Regardless of the answer, you need to be mindful that your goal in any presentation is to get to the next step.

You should quantify the problem whenever possible.

"In your experience, can you tell me how often that happens here?"

"How much do you think that is costing you?"

"How much time does that take when you've done it in the past?"

Resist the tendency to present too soon. Some reps get so excited when they hear the slightest hint of an opportunity that they turn on the spigot of benefits. Hold off, ask a few more questions, get better information, and you're able to craft an even harder-hitting description of benefits, tailored precisely to what they're interested in increasing your credibility.

Again, you should only talk about your product/service after knowing specifically how it will solve the problem, meet their need, etc. Then you can tailor your remarks specifically and personally because you already know what interests them.

Avoid the question, "Anything else?" when attempting to up sell.

Just like when a fast food clerk asks the same question, the answer is usually, "No."

Instead, give them a suggestion, and help them answer. For example, after they agree to buy an item, or a service, say, "Many of our other clients who purchased _____ also find that _____ is also something that makes sense for them."

The concept of "buyer fingerprints" is one of the simplest yet profound techniques that were ever taught to me by Dr. Donald Moine.

One of the questions that I teach to my clients in the real estate industry is, "Tell me, are you looking for the ideal home in a nice quiet neighborhood?"

This question opens up the floodgates of information when you have helped them created a picture of the ideal home in a nice quiet neighborhood. The follow-up question is "Can you tell me what that looks like?"

The key to persuading your prospect is motivation. Every human being is motivated by something. Your job is to find out what motivates your prospect and then to fulfill that motivation.

People have two major motivations: the desire for gain and the fear of loss. The desire for gain motivates people to want more of the things they value in life. They want more money, more success, more health, more influence, more respect, more love and more happiness.

The fear of loss appeals to the selfish aspect of people. They do not want to lose out on losing something that they have already.

Human wants are limited only by individual imagination. No matter how much a person has, he or she still wants more and more. When you can show a person how he or she can get more of the things he or she wants by helping you achieve your goals, you can motivate them to act in your behalf.

You will learn more by asking rather than telling.

Chapter 9:
Closing Skills And Strategies

We mentioned this concept in an earlier chapter; The One-Third Rule. There is a general rule of thumb in sales, as taught to me by America's number one corporate trainer, Stephan Schiffman. He told me that:

1/3 of the qualified people you talk to <u>will</u> buy from you.

1/3 of the qualified people you talk to will <u>never</u> buy from you.

1/3 of the qualified people you talk to <u>may</u> buy from you <u>depending</u> on what you say or do.

See, order-takers, or the average salespeople snap up the first 1/3 and they may make an okay living. The problem is that they have to find that 1/3. Most times, they cannot find that 1/3 they need to in order to make their major pay check. They will never rise above their comfort level.

Closing is an attitude. It is not an event or a transition into the "battle phase".

Question: When should you try to close?
Most schools of thought suggest closing when you feel that all of the prospects' concerns and objections have been met. I disagree. Ben Gay, III, the author of "The Closers" series of books taught me different. His strategies are profound in their simplicity.

Ever watched that movie with Alec Baldwin, Ed Harris, Kevin Spacey, Jack Lemmon and Al Pacino... "Glengarry Glen Ross"?

Alec Baldwin's character says," A...B...C... Always Be Closing. A... Always... B... Be... C... Closing"

You should be closing all the time. From the very start, after you have qualified the prospect, everything in your script should be designed for closing. I am not talking about "kicking, scratching and clawing your way" to writing the order up.

You should start closing from the time you say "hello".
We are not talking about saying this from the very start, "Hi, I'm Chris. Are you going to buy today?"

Its really creating that positive first impression, answering their questions, needs and wants, making them feel comfortable, so when it comes time to say "Here, sign this.", you've **earned** the right to close. Moreover, closing can be as simple as saying "this makes sense to me, how about you?"

You should be closing all the time with trial closes, with asking questions and definitely when the prospect is ready to buy!

Now that we have settled that, let's talk about HOW to close. Many salespeople breeze through the presentation with extreme confidence, and come to a screeching halt when they try to ask for the sale.

Remember, you have qualified the prospect; you know that he will derive benefit from your service and you have demonstrated that you sincerely want to help him. If you have laid the proper groundwork, there is no huge secret to close the sale. Simply ask for it"

"Let's get the paperwork started so that we can deliver by next week."

"Let's write it up. When would you like the service to start?"

"You really need this... Why don't you give it a try?"

"Just try it. I know you'll be pleasantly surprised with the results."

More closing techniques:

a.   To Ask!

b.   Alternative Choice

c.   Drop Sell

d.   Take Away The Risk

e.   Reduce To The Ridiculous

f.   Free Trial

g.   The Nudge

h.   Down Payment/Finance

i.   Future Commitment

j.   If Your Spouse Says "NO, You Can Cancel.

k.   If You Were To...

An example of how to use each one:

a.   The most important thing you can do to close a sale is to ask for the order. Most times people want to buy, but they are sometimes afraid of saying so. They are waiting for you, the sales professional to make the first move.

b.   "Would you like to write a check for this or would you rather put this on your card?"
"We can deliver this out to you as early as Thursday, or would Monday be okay for you?"

c.   "We have a model with without the extra bells and whistles, would that work out better for you?"

d.   "We stand behind our product. We offer a 100% money back guarantee. If you are not happy for nay reason, we will give you your money back. Since we take all of the financial risk and take it off of your shoulders, let's go ahead and right this up."

e.   "This model is an extra $60 a month. That is like 2 sodas a day. If you gave up 2 sodas a day, you could afford it, couldn't you?"

f.   "Just authorize right here and you'll get to try this out for 30 days with no obligation whatsoever"

g.   "You know this is going to help you out and increase your employees' efficiency. Why don't you just try it out?"

h.   "If we were able to start you off with a small down payment and affordable monthly investments, you'd want to do this, right?"

i.   "I understand you don't have it in the budget right now. How about this; we'll deliver it now so you can start using it, and we'll only start billing you for it next quarter, fair enough?

j.   "Why don't you go ahead and get this first. If after talking it over with your wife, and if she absolutely, positively doesn't agree with your decision, we'll go ahead and cancel the contract, is that fair?"

k.   "If you were to save money, increase efficiency and streamline the process, you'd want to get this wouldn't you?"

Practice these closes. Script out various ways of saying them as it applies to your industry, product and personality. Role-play so that it becomes natural for you. You do not have to remember a thousand different techniques. All you have to do is earn the right to close by taking your prospect down the path of making an intelligent and informed decision, and they will say yes.

PART B: MINDSET

Chapter 10:
Characteristics of A Sales Professional

It always amazes me when salespeople trying to get me as a client forget my name or they forget information that I have given them in prior meetings.

One of the attributes I have worked really hard on is improving my memory. Through countless hours of practice and determination, I am able to remember names and faces. One of the biggest compliments I get is that I have a great memory. It is very impressive when you are able to recall information.

Keeping records is extremely vital to the business of selling. You may think that you might not have enough time to make proper notes.

However, if you are spending precious time searching your memory for facts and figures, you are on the losing end of the scale. Use technology to help you remember things.

Carry a notebook (with a pen!) everywhere you go. Better yet, use a voice recorder. That way, you can record notes and ideas on the spot and put them on paper at the end of the day. Write notes on your prospects at the end of every call.

Make it a habit to write at least twenty words about the phone call when it has ended. This will allow you to remember items that you probably would have forgotten the next time you called them.

Do you really understand what you are selling? Specifically, are you familiar describing your product or service in intimate detail? Learn as much as you possibly can about your product or service. Use it in exactly the same way that a client would.

This gives you first-hand experience about what you are selling. It is very much easier to make statements that you can stand confidently behind.

This gives you enthusiasm about your product. I am not talking about going on and on about your service like a blithering idiot. Some prospects need to hear the technical details.

Others want to hear all about what your service will do for them. Be sure to find out exactly what your prospects' hot buttons are and concentrate there.

I have seen many salespeople lie, especially over the phone. I am a firm believer that you cannot cheat long enough when dealing with people over the phone to make it worth the effort in the long run.

Your prospect will pick up on your insincerity. You cannot run from it. Doing that gives all professional telephone salespeople a bad name. Don't do it! If you know that a potential client will not derive any benefit from the service, do not sell it to him.

A short time ago, I received a phone call from a telemarketer identifying himself as a representative from my bank. Upon listening to his pitch, I found out that he was not calling from my bank at all! His company was only an affiliate partner of the bank.

He had started the call under the cover of deceit. I asked him why he misrepresented himself. He told me that is what he was told to say and it was in the script. Needless to say, he did not make a sale. There is no reason to misrepresent. It is time to move on when your company tells you to lie.

A question I ask in my workshops is, "How many of you agree that knowledge is power?"

Invariably, almost everyone agrees with this statement. I then ask everyone if they agree that fast food is not the healthiest thing they can put in their bodies. I usually get a resounding agreement.

I then ask the audience how many of them have visited fast food restaurant at least once in the last 10 days. At this point, I usually get some people shamefacedly raising their hands and others chuckling at themselves.
We know that it is not healthy, yet we *still* do it.

You see, the point behind is that knowledge is not power. Applied knowledge is power. What good is knowledge if you do not use it? What good are all the support, techniques and strategies if you do not get yourself to do these things?
We all know what we are supposed to do. Many of us have the problem of simply not doing it. We will talk about this in more detail in Chapter 15: "Feeling vs. Action".

All the knowledge and skills that you have should be applied. Do not just think about it; do not just consider using these skills. Use them to get better results!

Let's go into the characteristics of sales professionals.

1. Sales professionals know what they want and reject any activities that do not help them in achieving their goals.

2. Sales professionals pay attention to the big picture, at the same time; they also pay attention to the necessary day-to-day activities.

3. Sales professionals create a success environment, staying away from negative influences.

4. Sales professionals endure uncertainty and chaos.

5. Sales professionals avoid stress-related problems.

6. Sales professionals manage their emotions.

7. Sales professionals know how to delegate, network and co-operate.

8. Sales professionals understand and practice the principles of human understanding and communication.

9. Sales professionals are passionate about their work.

10. Sales professionals are competitive.

11. Sales professionals are aware of their comfort zones and are not afraid to stretch themselves to get out of their comfort zones.

12. Sales professionals prefer to solve problems rather than place blame.

13. Sales professionals visualize positive results.
14. Sales professionals analyze their performance.

15. Sales professionals write out, review and work towards their goals.

16. Sales professionals strive to improve their product knowledge.

17. Sales professionals practice their craft.

18. Sales professionals ask relevant, pertinent, and intelligent questions.

19. Sales professionals are great listeners.

20. Sales professionals create and nurture quality relationships with their prospects and clients.

As a sales professional, think about how you would like to be treated, especially by others in the sales profession. The way we treat other salespeople is an indication of how we feel about ourselves in this profession.

Our profession is what makes the economy go around. Nothing happens until a salesperson sells something.

In every company, every position serves an important function. What people sometimes forget is that the salaries are paid through revenue; revenue generated by the salespeople in the company.

I remember a very interesting experience. I walked into a real estate office to conduct a group presentation for an upcoming seminar we were conducting in the area. The presentation was to the real state agents in a rather large franchise here in Southern California.

The manager of the office greeted me in the lobby in a very courteous and professional manner. So far so good.

He brings me to the lunchroom and offers me coffee, bread rolls and cake. I accept water (need to watch my weight, remember!).

On my way back to the conference room, I passed an agent in the hallway from the other direction. We nod, smile and introduce ourselves to each other. He tells me his name; I tell him mine, mention my company name and the reason why I am in their office. I said, "I'm here to conduct a sales workshop and also to let everyone know about a powerful sales seminar we're doing at the convention center."

What he says next surprises the heck out of me! He looks at me with something bordering on disgust, snarls, "Get out of here!", and he walks off.

Why did he do that?

Generally, people look down on salespeople and there are many in the sales profession that are ashamed of what they do for a living.

Selling is a noble profession. The economy revolves around selling. Nothing happens until something is sold by a sales professional. Look around. Someone sold everything you see.

Be proud of what you do.

Chapter 11:
How To Set And Achieve Any Goal

I believe that goal setting is a skill. Now, there are some that believe that it is an art. I say "hogwash"! It is a skill that can be learned.

It is a skill that you can use to achieve ANYTHING you set your mind to, whether good, bad, legal, illegal, moral, immoral, facetious, or altruistic. Of course, I am only being facetious. We only encourage good goals!

If you do not have clear goals, the future looks hazy and ill defined, and you only wish for things to be different. It has been said that a dream is a goal without a clear action plan and deadline.

When you do not have a clear destination, you are often all dressed up with nowhere to go. You may have some success, but lack real progress in any direction. Without clear goals, you may never live up to your full potential because you do not put in 100% of your effort because it is just not that important.

Without clear goals, you think that your life could or should be better, but you just do not know how.

An individual I used to work for shared this experience with me; he was helping a friend of his move and they were clearing out a hallway closet when they cam across a stack of his old journals.

They looked through them and read through a few pages of goals his friend had written out a few years ago. Turns out his friend had achieved every single one of his goals he had written out!

He told his friend that he must be pretty happy since he had achieved all of his goals over the last couple of years. His friend replied that not only was he not happy, in fact, he was downright pissed off!

WHY?

His reply, "If I had known I was going to achieve all of my goals, I would have written BIGGER GOALS!"

There is something powerful about the written word. It makes our thoughts and feelings a reality when we put them on paper.

I used to love to eat (and my wife would say that I still do!) In fact, I ate so much; I used to weigh around 317lbs. In 4 years, I had put on almost 120 lbs! I was a heifer.

I was always telling myself that I wanted to lose the weight. I really wished I weighed less. I dreamed of being able to wear my nice clothes again. But I did not do anything. I did not do anything for about 2 years. It was all talk with no action. My solution to the problem was to buy bigger clothes.

Then, one of my most brilliant mentors, Dr. Donald Moine, PhD, shared a strategy with me that has helped me achieve every goal I put through his strategy. I loved it so much I added an initial step.

1. Determine your reason(s) why you want this outcome.
2. Establish your ultimate outcome with a date of accomplishment.
3. Develop a superior strategy
4. Implement the strategy with massive action.

In a simple expression:

WHY > WHAT > HOW & WHEN > DO IT

Step 1 and 2 could be interchangeable; you can come up with either one first. A famous quote states that for positive change to occur, dissatisfaction must be evident or present.

I had an outcome, but there was no date attached to it because I had not identified my "reason why" I wanted to realize this goal.

A while ago, I had to make a business trip to Malaysia. The plane ride was almost a total of 18 hours in the air.

When I got on the plane and getting myself settled in my seat, I was trying to wear my seat belt. Because of my extensive girth, you see.

While I was trying to do this, a PYT (pretty young thing) flight attendant came over, leaned in to me and helpfully said, "Sir, would you like an extension for your seat belt?"

"An extension for my seat belt?" I thought to myself, "You've got to be joking!"

I sucked my gut in, cinched the seat belt, clicked it in, and wheezed, "No, thank you".

It was about a 14-hour plane ride. This became one of my reasons why I needed to lose the weight. I would never allow anyone to ask me if I needed an extension for my seat belt ever again.

On the way back, however, I asked for one because I could not take that again!

So here is how my four steps looked like:

1.   I will weigh 195lbs by Dec 31st 2006.

2.   I will achieve this goal because of the following reasons:

3.   My action plan:

i.   I will cut down my food intake by at least 20%

ii.   I will ride my bike 3 times a week for a minimum of 30 minutes each time.

4. Implementation

Using these steps, with 7 months to go before my deadline, I am about 55lbs away from achieving this goal. I have absolutely no doubt that I will achieve that goal.

There are some categories of goals that you should identify. To help you along, I have some suggested areas to help you along.

Feel free to create and add some of your categories:

1. Personal
2. Business
3. Career
4. Financial
5. Relationship
6. Spiritual
7. Life Achievement
8. Health
9. Fitness
10. Mental
11. Educational
12. Environmental

We had a client named Kathy and she works in a very glamorous industry.

She sells paper boxes. She had been doing that for about three years and her monthly average check was about $6,000. $6,000 a month for three years. Not too shabby.

When we started a coaching relationship with her, one of the first things we did was put her through this goal setting process and helped her create, define and implement her action plan.

So her goal was to double her income. So she had been making $6,000 a month and now all of a sudden, she wanted to jump to $12,000 a month. Pretty big goal, huh?

When she did not tell us was that she secretly increased her goal from $12,000 to $30,000. She said if she was going to get crazy, she was going to go all the way.

So Kathy followed her action plan very well. Can you guess what her next month's check was? She made $6,000 again! She failed in her goal. Can you guess what she made the next month after that?

Well, she failed again... she only made $27,800. However, did she cry about it? Heck no. She was ecstatic. Interesting isn't it?

Let me introduce a plan that's called the G.I.A.P. (Goal Identification and Achievement Process). It consists of a series of steps that you take in order to achieve any goal that you set your mind on.

A question that you should be asking yourself is, "If I absolutely knew that I was going to achieve my goal, what would my actions be today?"

Step 1
Identify the 5 most important goals that you want to accomplish over the next 90 days and write them down individually. These could be anything that you want to achieve

over the next 90 days, be it personal, professional, religious or financial.

Step 2
Identify the reason that you want to accomplish each goal and write each reason down. These reasons have to be strong enough to help you weather and overcome the challenges that will come up in your journey to achieve these goals.

Step 3
Write down a list of all the action steps that must be done in order to accomplish each goal. Anything that comes to mind, write it down, because writing something down make it come to life.

Step 4
Rewrite the list of action steps, prioritizing the action steps for each of the goals that you have come up with.

Step 5
Make a written plan of action: You may choose to simply do the action steps for each goal in the prioritized order and have that as your plan of action. When you actually begin to write out a plan of action I am sure that you will find other things that you did not think of when you listed your action steps.

Step 6
View your goals on daily basis: Get at least five 5 x 7 index cards and write all five of your goals on each note card in big bold letters with a marker. Post these goal cards in places where you see them on a regular basis. I would suggest these locations; bathroom mirror, bedroom mirror, refrigerator, dashboard of your car and your workstation.

Step 7
Speak your goals out loud several times a day: Words have TREMENDOUS power. We have the power to speak things into existence. Speak your goals out loud 5 - 10 times a day. When

you speak your goals, speak them with power and belief. Get excited about the things that you are going to accomplish over the next 90 days. Because it is going to happen!

Step 8
Visualize your goals on a daily basis: (Example: See yourself in your mind's eye accomplishing your goals. Think about how great it will feel to succeed in this area of your life.

Visualize these things on a daily basis, believe and see yourself accomplishing your goals. I want you to imagine what it will feel like when your goal becomes a reality and your dreams come true!

Step 9
Share your goals with others: Find positive minded people who will support your success and share your goals with them. Stay away from the negative people that will simply discourage you, or laugh at you and hold you back.

Step 10
Get an accountability partner. Find someone who is success minded and goal oriented and make yourselves accountable to each other. Commit to email your daily schedule to each other each day along with a progress report of the current day's activities.

Be ready to offer advice, encouragement and motivation to your accountability partner. Be ready and open to receiving the same.

Step 11
Review your goals on a weekly basis. It is not only important to see your goals on a regular basis, it is just as important to remind yourself of the reason that you want to accomplish your goals and the action you must take in order to accomplish your goals. It is also important to review your actions each day to make sure you are staying on track with your plan.

Ask yourself this question: ***Are my actions consistent with my goals?***

If your actions are not consistent with your goals, change your actions!

Follow this structured plan diligently and you'll achieve whatever goal you've set your sights on.

Chapter 12:
Time Management For Sales Professionals

There are 1440 minutes every single day. Whether you use them or not, they are gone. There is nothing anyone can do about it. You can spend all your money, or you can lose it all and you can always make it back. But if you waste even one minute, you can never get it back.

Do you know what the significance of 29,930 is?

If you take that number and divide it by 365, you get 82. That is the average life span of a human being in a modern, developed country. That puts everything in perspective, doesn't it? You have an average of 29,930 days to be on this earth.

Wanna hear something frightening? Whatever your age is, minus it from 82, and divide that by 365. That is the number of days you have left. If you are 40 years old, you will have 15,330 days left to make it count.

If there were a way to get more stuff done, be more productive and accomplish more with less effort, you'd be very interested in that, wouldn't you? Of course you would!

The first thing you want to remember is that you want to focus on is "Active" versus "Productive". To be active is undertaking "busy" work without any real work being accomplished. It is activity without results.

What does being "productive" really mean? It means accomplishing something of substance, doesn't it? It means getting the job done and achieving a result.

Which would you rather be; Active or Productive? Of these two, which has the higher chance of contributing towards success?

Most people believe that one of our most important assets is TIME. There are also others that believe that TIME is a great liability. I suggest to you that you have the ability of choosing if TIME is a liability or an asset.

Salespeople are hired to basically do four things:

a. Prospect

b. Make presentations

c. Close sales

d. Ask for referrals

As sales professionals, there is a whole range of activities and responsibilities that go into these large categories. There is filing, paperwork, office meetings, sales meetings, going for classes or training, socializing, and families.

A great way to decide which activity is a priority is to assign a dollar value to your time. So, if you make $50,000 a year, working 40 hours a week, your hourly wage translates to $26.04. If you earn $100,000 a year, your hourly rate is $52.08.

With these figures in mind, you can decide if the activity is worth your time at that moment. Ask yourself this question; "Will this activity give me $26 worth of result?

Knowing this breakdown, you should be concentrating on generating revenue. Do the paperwork, the filing and the non revenue-producing activities after the "golden hours" of talking to prospects.

I was taught the value of time reinforced with real human experiences. To fully understand the true value of time...

One YEAR	- ask a student who has to repeat a grade
One MONTH	- ask the mother of a premature baby
One WEEK	- ask the salesperson that missed his prospect who went on vacation
One DAY	- ask the man who forgot an anniversary.
One HOUR	- two lovers about to be apart
One MINUTE	- ask a person that missed their flight
One SECOND	- ask a person that just missed an accident
A MILISECOND	- ask the Olympic athlete that came in second

Top 10 Time Wasters

1. Inadequate planning
2. Telephone/drop-in interruptions
3. Taking on too much
4. Not delegating
5. Can't say NO
6. Procrastination
7. Meetings
8. Administrative paperwork
9. Miscommunication
10. Disorganization

Time-Saving Techniques

1. Learn how to say NO

2.   Be Proactive vs. Reactive

3.   Avoid Time Wasters

4.   Use technology

5.   Hire an assistant

6.   Create systems

7.   Block out time – Power of 10

8.   Set time limits

9.   Plan Everything On Paper

When you learn how to say "No" to people and projects that do not contribute to your personal production, you will find that there is going to be more time you can devote to revenue-generating activities.

When you plan out your day and prioritize your activities, you can roll with the flow of the day. You determine what needs to be done, instead of always reacting to situations that come up and "making do". You will have a clear idea of how the day is supposed to go.

Avoid time-wasters like a long lunch. Or people popping in your office wanting to chat about last night's episode of "Fear Factor". Your time is valuable. Use it wisely.

When I have conversations during office, especially with my staff, my first question, if I am calling them is: "I need 2 minutes to talk to you, can we do it now?" Or when they call me, my question then becomes, "How long do you need this conversation to be?"

This way, everyone is mindful of the time and a valuable resource is not wasted talking about things not pertinent at the time.

Use technology to help you manage your time. You can automate your email newsletters so that they can be done automatically. Send a fax from your computer instead of writing or typing them out, then printing them and then walking over to the fax machine and watching the fax go through. Make a list of all the technological help that you can get to get things done faster.

If you have calculated what you are worth an hour, and if it is over $30, you should hire an assistant. Alternatively, you could get together with a like-minded person in your office and you could both hire an assistant to handle all of the filing, paperwork, routine calls and typing for the both of you. Your time is too valuable to do your own filing. Or you could hire your kids, if they are old enough to help you out part-time.

You should create systems to streamline your work. Fr example, in my business, after we set an appointment, we send out a confirmation fax. Everyone that receives the fax gets the same one except it has their name on it.

We created this fax over two years ago, and except for minor adjustments, we have continued to send it out without having to create a different fax each time. And of course, we fax it through the computer which saves even more time!

The Power of 10 is a very simple strategy. It focuses on carrying out an activity, such as checking your email and answering them, with no interruptions for a concentrated period of time, that is, 10 minutes. The beauty of the Power of 10 is that you can block out several of these per day for different activities.

We talked about every day having 1440 minutes. Ask yourself these questions when planning your day.

* What must I accomplish today?

- Who do I need to follow-up with?

- What appointments do I have today?

- Activities that need block time.

- What can I delegate today?

- What can I reschedule for tomorrow?

I share with my clients a philosophy that states, "What doesn't get scheduled doesn't get done". Salespeople that say they cannot fit in training or cannot go on vacation because they have too much work constantly amaze me. If they have too much work that they cannot take a vacation or spend time with their family, they are in the wrong business.

One of the attractions of a sales position is that you control your own time. Using strategies of time management, you should be able to organize your life such that you are able to schedule in other things in life that are important.

Remember what your time is worth and focus on the activities that will produce the greatest amount of return for your time.

Chapter 13:
Overcoming Fear & Procrastination

"I am the greatest. I said that before I knew I was"
- Muhammad Ali

Two things constantly hold us back in our pursuit of success and happiness; fear and procrastination.

It is natural to have fear. It shows you are human. People have all kinds of fear. Fear of success, rejection, failure, spiders, people, closed spaces, public speaking.... And the list goes on.

The main causes of fear are:

1.   Lack of skill

2.   Poor self image

3.   Approval from others

4.   Negative self talk

You see, when you lack the skills you lack confidence. You will experience fear when you lack confidence. What do you need to know about your product or service that would make you more confident? What do you need to learn about your prospects and customers so that you can sell them better? If you were able to learn all these things, that would make you a better salesperson, won't it?

When you have a poor self-image, you do not really see yourself as an expert who can solve problems. Your customers will need to see you as a problem solver. You are there to offer a solution to their needs.

If you have a poor self-image, your prospects will not see you as the bearer of good news. It has been proven that you cannot teach people to do anything that conflicts with their self-image.

People can only perform in a manner that is consistent with how they see themselves.

However, you can improve your self-image. It is imperative that you see yourself as the expert in your field and that you have the information that will benefit your clients. A strong positive self-image is what makes all the techniques in this book work.

Every person wants to be liked. We look for approval in all of our relationships. We have done this at an early age. We have been conditioned in this manner throughout our upbringing. We seek approval from our friends, parents, siblings, teachers, coworkers and bosses.

We have learned that when we do something that meets with approval we are rewarded. The constant need to be liked is ingrained in all of us. And there is nothing wrong with that at all. We do have to realize that in our chosen profession, we are going to be rejected. We will not obtain approval 100% of the time.

We have to remember that when the people do not behave the way that we want them to we should not become upset or feel rejected.

If we allow this to affect us, if further causes us to perform poorly. You cannot win all the time. You cannot sell everyone all the time. You do have to try, though!

You should expect running into resistance when dealing with prospects. Hoping for prospects to greet you with open arms and being ready to buy is absolutely unrealistic and ridiculous. It is our job to make them comfortable. It is not their job to make us comfortable.

You probably will come across the buyers that will whip out their checkbook and buy what you have simply because of the timing.

They may have woken up this morning thinking to themselves, "I need to buy _____ today."

This does not happen often enough though. So just tell yourself that you will give 100% in every encounter and the numbers will take care of themselves.

Sometimes we are our own worst critic. We all have a little voice that talks to us. We have enormous control over our emotions if we work hard at controlling them and if we practice saying the right things to ourselves.

Oftentimes, we tell ourselves that we are not going to make it. We tell ourselves we are going to fail. For example:

"I hate cold calling"

"That will never work"

"I'm going to fail"

"There going to tell me no"

"I'm bothering them"

"They won't have time"

"I'll never hit the quota"

The answer to this is very simple. We should program our little voice to be positive. You can do that by programming positive self-talk into your psyche.

The human mind is a fascinating machine. The interesting thing about the human mind is that it does not differentiate between a real and an imagined event.

The mind will believe something that you tell it over and over again. So if you speak positive words your mind will believe the positive words.

Your mind will take in this information and reprogram itself to your advantage.

You tell yourself that you are the expert in your field.

"I am great at cold calling"

"I will exceed my quota"

"I solve my clients' problems"

Fear causes us to procrastinate, among other factors. The actions that we take are normally influenced by how we feel. So, in essence, how we feel influences how we act. What we need to do is separate our feelings from our actions. When we are able to separate our actions from our feelings, we will be able to do what we are supposed to.

During my seminars and workshops, I usually share that one of my fears is standing in front of a group of people and talking to them. I usually get looks of surprise and disbelief when the audience hears this.

I have had to work extremely hard to overcome this fear that has held me back for literally decades. It was so bad that when I was in school, it make me sick to my stomach when they were taking attendance, because I had to say "present" out loud when my name was called.

When I was in the service, after boot camp, they sent me to Officer Candidate School. The instructors there were called mentors. At the tender age of 17, I did not know what a "mentor" was. I did know that they were really, really good at drawing out our fears and weaknesses and helping us overcome them. After a couple of weeks, we figured it out; it stood for "mental torture".

In one of the training exercises, we had a tower; it kind of looked like the Eiffel Tower, except it was only two stories tall. What we had to do was run up to the second story, go up to the edge and jump off. We had buddies down below holding a tarp, which we would land on to break our fall.

When it was my turn, I stepped to the edge and I thought to myself "Chris, I think you're afraid of heights, so you're not going to jump". So I stepped to the side and I let everyone else go.

Pretty soon, I was the last one. Not a good position to be in. The mentors told me to jump and I said "no". I was stuck up there for about 15 minutes and they finally threatened me with something that made me more afraid of them than I was of jumping.

So I jumped and I landed safely on the tarp. I felt good that I had done it and I was ecstatic!

Guess what happened next?

They made me go again and again. I jumped another 30 times by myself in the next 45 minutes.

After this experience, was I still afraid of heights? Heck yes!

But you know what? It was because of this exercise that I was able to jump out of a plane 52 times!

You see, to me, courage is not the absence of fear; it's in spite of.

When we face our fears, we tend to realize that it is not that bad. I have clients that are in real estate and they use a method of prospecting called "farming". It is when they work a particular neighborhood by introducing themselves to the homeowner. They tell me that they walk confidently up the driveway, knock purposefully on the door...and they hope that nobody's home!

In your industry, you have had similar experience, haven't you? So what can you do to overcome fear?

Practice

Repetition

Knowledge

Other's Experience

Setting your "purpose" goals

You have picked a challenging yet rewarding career. Many have tried and given up in this career. Remember this: "If it was easy, everybody would be doing it".

A famous quote states it easy to pay the price if the promise is clear. Let's hear it again. It is easy to pay the price if the promise is clear.

Thousands upon thousands of sales are lost every single day simply because salespeople are afraid or reluctant to ask for the order. They are afraid to ask for a larger order, afraid to ask the prospect to take action NOW, instead of "tomorrow", "next week" and so on.

Sometimes we convince ourselves that we have more to do than time to do it in. Putting things off is the surefire way to make sure things never get done. Have you ever felt that organizing your files was more important than picking up the phone to make your next call?

Let me share a secret with you. Salespeople are not paid to organize files or straighten their work areas. Salespeople are paid to close sales.

I have never been able to close a prospect when shifting files around. Amazingly, the only time a sale is closed is when you are talking to a prospect. Get rid of this deadly habit.

Start each day by making a list of things that have to be done on that day. Then proceed with working on that list. This system will help prevent you from shoving unpleasant tasks to the bottom of the list where they will eventually be forgotten.

Chapter 14:
No Such Thing As Bulletproof Psychology

We are all put to test throughout our lives; But hardly ever the form or the time that we prefer. That is life.

You often hear so-called experts talk about bulletproof psychology. I believe there is no such thing. The reason I say that is because we are human beings with emotions. Sometimes we are not able to control them immediately.

Actually, I have been told that there are people that possess bulletproof psychology. You can find them in the asylum.

In the world of professional athletes, dedicated professionals focus on conditioning their bodies in preparation for "game day". In practice, they will go over their moves and rehearse their plays over and over again. They do this with the intention of achieving perfection in their profession.

But is there such thing as perfection? I do not know. I do know that I have heard, "I'm not perfect, I'm human".

So why do we strive for perfection? I believe that perfection is a state of mind. And if you allow yourself to believe that, you will do it and do it well, then that is darn near perfect!

Using the athletes as an example again, they not only focus on their physical aspects, they will religiously devote time and attention to their minds, or belief.

Take two sports teams (the sport does not matter, so just pick your favorite). If all things being equal; strength, stamina, then the team that BELIEVES and KNOWS they're going win will edge out the team that HOPES to win. Do you see the difference?

What we believe we can do is sometimes as important as or more important than what our skill level is.

Do you believe you can or you cannot? Either way, you are right!

Rejection is a pretty strong negative emotion. Remember the first time you asked a girl out on a date? What were you most afraid of? That she would say NO? We get dejected when we are rejected! The very nature of people is to seek approval. When someone shuts us down, we take it personally. As a professional salesperson, you cannot do that.

There is no profession in the world where we get as much rejection as in professional selling. This is especially the case on the telephone because of the sheer numbers of people that we talk to. So, you might as well get used to it. The real question is; are there ways around it?

The first thing you should realize is that professional selling is a numbers game. It is a game of statistics. To succeed at it, you need to know what the numbers are.

I am going to suggest a strategy that is extremely simple to implement. If you diligently implement this system, you will take a huge leap in increasing your results and your income.

You will see a dramatic improvement in your results in a couple of short weeks. I will use the scenario of making cold calls on the telephone. However, you can use this system whatever your sales process is.

Get a notepad and make four columns: Number of Dials, Left Message, Completed Calls, Presentations, Number of Closes (or Appointments Set).

i.   Number of Dials. Each time your fingers dial a number, place a tic in this column. This means that a wrong number, getting an answering machine, a disconnected number message or successfully reaching the number that you dialed qualifies under this column.

ii.   Left Message. In this column, any instance of reaching a prospect's voicemail, answering machine or leaving you details with a receptionist goes into this column.

iii.   Completed Calls. Each time you reach your prospect or decision-maker, give yourself a credit in this column.

iv.   Presentations. Every time you hold an intelligent, legitimate conversation with a prospect about your service, give yourself a credit in this column.

v.   Number of Closes. Every time you make a sale (or make an appointment, if that is the aim of the call), give yourself a credit in this column.

At the end of the day, add the numbers up. Keep these daily numbers until you have collected two weeks worth of data. These numbers tell a story. They tell a sales story. These numbers will help you understand how well you are doing and will show you where you need to focus your attention on.

For example, you see that it takes 100 dials to make 60 completed calls, to make 30 presentations, to close 6 sales. For most salespeople, to see an increase in results and ultimately income, you can focus on three areas:

a.   Sell to more prospects

b.   Sell more to each prospect

c.   Sell more often to clients

The easiest area to focus on initially is a) Sell to more prospects. When you chart the numbers, according to the above example, the ratio is **100 dials: 6 sales**.

If you want to improve your income and increase your sales to 8, what should you do? Make 134 dials. Or to look at the numbers a different way, with 60 completed calls, the number of sales closed is 6. The ratio is **60 completed calls: 6 sales**.

To achieve 8 sales, the calls you should complete are 80. To complete 80 calls, you need to make 134 dials. Numbers do not lie. They tell the story of success or failure.

To overcome the feeling of rejection, when we analyze the above numbers, we find that you close a sale for every 17 dials. It takes an average of 16 NOs before you get a YES.

This system shows you that every step you take along your daily routine is important. You may not have thought that leaving a message or counting the number of completed dials as contributing towards your income. Every dial works in your favor. Some are going to slip away.

Remember this adage;

"Some Will... Some Won't... So What... NEXT!"

When you know that rejection is going to come, you do not have to take it personally. You may not want to focus on the reject rate, but you should, at the very least, determine what it is. Once you have identified your calling numbers, you can set your own goals and figure out the best ways of achieving them.

Emotional Cycles
Most salespeople make hundreds of calls a week, if not a day. Or they meet several prospects in a day. They say pretty much the same things over and over again with some variations.

There is a constant challenge to keep the repetitive nature of the calls from lowering the quality of each call. Remember that a new prospect would have never heard your presentation before. To him it is the first time. Do not spoil it for him.

In addition, as you are making your calls throughout the day, keep in tune with how you are feeling. Is there a time when you seem to be banging your head against the wall? Maybe it is the first few calls of the day. Or after lunch time, or just before the end of your day? Whatever the case is, you need to identify it before you can fix it.

I knew a salesperson that would stop calling right around 4pm. He would say, "No point calling. All my prospects are thinking about going home right now. If I called them, they would just say to call back in the morning. I'm gonna call it a day".

This was a mental block. His mind found the perfect reason why he could not sell after 4pm. This self-prophecy prevented him from ever making a sale after 4pm.

Change negative patterns. Spend your time eliminating negatives and concentrate on increasing the positives.

Laziness
It makes absolutely no difference how well you make your presentation, answer an objection or close the sale. If you do not make the necessary number of calls, you will fail.

How many calls should you make in a day? That depends on how many you CAN make in a day. Remember, nothing happens until you pick that phone up. If you do not pick up the phone, there is absolutely no chance that you will make that sale.

You never have to experience rejection again. After all, what is rejection? It is not an experience; it is your definition of the experience. So, ensure that you accomplish something on each call, and you can hold your head high with a sense of achievement.

Remember, for a sales professional, a decision of any type is better than shadow-chasing someone who will waste your time with wimpy or misleading statements that cause you to believe there's a chance, when, in fact, there's not

A good way to end a call where you do not accomplish your primary objection (and to never experience rejection) is to plant a seed for the future. Give them something to look for, based upon what you uncovered during the call . . . something that might just cause them to call you back.

For example, "Pat, it looks like we don't have a fit here, today, but I suggest that if you ever find yourself needing an emergency job finished, and don't have the staff to handle it, give us a call. We specialize in those types of projects, and would love to talk to you."

Everyone has been surprised by those written-off prospects who later called to order. This is a way to proactively make it happen more often.

Listen to educational audio programs in your car. The average person drives 10,000 to 25,000 miles per year, which works out to, between 500 and 1000 hours per year that the average person spends in his or her car. You can become an expert in your field by simply listening to educational audio programs as you drive from place to place.

Attend seminars given by experts in your field. Take additional courses and learn everything you possibly can. Learn from the experts. Ask them questions, write them letters, read their books, read their articles and listen to people with proven records of accomplishment in the area in which you want to be successful

The last thing before you sleep and the first thing in the morning think about and visualize your goals as realities. See your goal as though it already existed.

Affirmations and pictures that are received in the present tense only activate your subconscious mind. See your goal vividly just before you go to sleep. See yourself performing at your best. See the situations that you are facing working out exactly the way you want them to.

See yourself living the kind of life that you want to live. See yourself with the kind of relationships, the kind of health, the kind of car, the kind of home you really want. Visualize all of these positive images just before you fall asleep at night.

The first thing you do when you get up in the morning is to feed yourself mental pictures. Those are the two times of the day when your subconscious mind is most receptive to new programming, when you fall asleep and when you wake up.

Here are two things you can do, all day long, to keep your mind and emotions focused on your goals and financial success:

First, listen to audio programs in your car and when you travel around. Continue feeding your mind with a stream of high quality, educational, motivational material that moves you toward your goal.

Second, resolve to associate with positive, optimistic people most of the time. Get around winners and get away from negative people who criticize, condemn and complain. This can change your life as much as any other factor.

Give yourself a pat on the back. You are a sales professional!

Chapter 15:
Get More Done Using Feeling vs. Action

It has been said that the difference between greatness and mediocrity is that mediocre people and great people know what they should be doing, and great people do it instead of just thinking or talking about it.

Top sales professionals set themselves apart when they are interested in making themselves better at what they do. Their families depend on it.

One of the greatest things in the selling profession is that we do not have someone constantly looking over our shoulders. One of the worst things is that we do not have anyone looking over or shoulders to give us structure.

Think about what the one thing is holding you back from being great.

In our profession, we have choices.

First of all, let us figure out what "profession" really means. A profession is largely defined as a calling requiring specific and specialized knowledge obtained through long and intensive preparation and study.

Professionals in any industry have to adhere to a higher and more rigorous standard in order to practice their profession. That is why they are called professionals.

Professionals generally make a conscious decision when they have chosen the line they in. Professionals make sacrifices in time, money, and relationships in order to live their chosen profession.

A couple years ago, I was conducting a training seminar in Anaheim and my staff and I usually spend the night before any event at the hotel.

We have made it a tradition to hang out at the pool after dinner for a swim and take a dip in the Jacuzzi. It is very relaxing and therapeutic. You should try it as soon and as often as you can.

So anyway, we are at the pool that night and we met some Marines that had just come back from Iraq and were headed on home. They started telling us stories of their experiences in Iraq and how some of their friends had died. The stuff they shared with us had a profound effect on me.

I realized that in some professions, when you make a mistake, somebody gets badly hurt or worse, dies.

In the profession of selling, we have the choice to organize our desk and files, hang out at the water cooler, take a 2-hour lunch or visit the golf course. You can make a mistake or have a bad day. When you have a bad day at selling, nobody dies.

Can you imagine if a surgeon was in the operating room and he was having a bad day? If a Marine in a war zone is having a bad day, either he gets injured or killed or his buddy does.

Professionals such as these cannot have a bad day. Professionals study more and train harder than anyone else. That is why they have earned the right to call themselves professionals.

What if you created the mindset and made the choice to have a good day everyday. You could focus on your tasks a little better and achieve just a little bit more every single day.

My office and home is in San Diego. When we conduct trainings and seminars throughout Southern California, we normally drive to them. Sometimes these trainings start at eight o'clock in the morning. Some of these are anywhere from 50 to 130 miles away from us.

When the trainings start at 8am, it means I have to wake up anywhere from 4am to 6am. Sometimes when my alarm clock goes off at 4 in the morning, I think to myself "Crap! It is 4 in the morning, I should go back to sleep. I don't feel like getting out of my bed and hitting traffic for the next 3 hours!"

I am sure you have said that to yourself before, haven't you!

Sometimes our clients tell us when they set their alarm clocks the night before they get really ambitious! They tell themselves that they are going to get up at 5am, go for a run, come back, get breakfast ready, and read the papers over a leisurely cup of coffee. Yeah, right!

When the alarm goes off at 5am, guess what usually happens! That is right, the snooze! They hit that snooze button several times before they get up.

At any point during the day, you have a choice to make. Do I go back to bed or to I get out of it?

Make your choices count. Make good choices. Make productive choices. It is entirely possible to constantly and consistently have a good day one after another in our chosen profession.

I challenge you to make a decision to exercise your ability to make choices. You have the choice to be the kind of professional that you want to be.

One of my mentors taught me that the secret to achieving success is to visualize myself as already having achieved that success. Everyday, I tell myself that I am successful. I see myself enjoying the fruits of my success. Because I tell my mind that I am successful, my mind believes it to be true.

If you were to hire one of the coaches in my organization to help you with your production and sales activities, one of the first things that would happen is that we would help you identify your purpose in life. We will develop your PERSONAL MISSION.

This is the reason why you get out of bed without hitting hat snooze button ten times in a row. Simply put, it is your reason WHY you exist. This WHY helps keep you working hard throughout the day, the week, the month and the year.

Your WHY causes you to continue in the face of obstacles, challenges and adversity.

Arguably, one of the greatest athletes of our time (or at least mine!) is Michael Jordan. Almost everyone wants to be like Mike. Michael Jordan got to where he was through sheer hard work, perseverance and determination.

He would be the first one at practice and the last one to leave. While other players took off during the off-season, Michael would work on his game to be better than not only any other player out there, but also better than himself.

Michael pictured himself as the best. The actions that he took personified the level of commitment he had that led directly to his achievements and success.

Ask yourself this question: "If I displayed as much passion, determination and commitment as Michael Jordan in my business, what would my results be?

Picture yourself at where you want to be. Then imagine what it would feel like to be there. Let the positive emotions run through you. Create a clear picture in your mind.

Then ask yourself where you are at today. Decide if you are ready for the level of commitment and determination necessary to get you to that point. If you are ready, then decide that no matter what happens you will do what is necessary to achieve your future. Some questions to ask yourself:

1. Where am I now?

2. Am I happy with my current situation?

3. Do I believe I can achieve my goals?

4. Am I willing to pay the price necessary to achieve this?

5. Am I determined to work constantly and consistently towards my vision?

6. Am I ready to face the challenges and obstacles?

There are several reasons why salespeople fail:

1. Don't make enough calls.

2. Don't ask for the order enough.

3. They talk too much instead of listening.

4. They don't plan.

5. They don't ask for referrals.

6. They don't set goals.

7. They focus on the wrong activities that don't contribute to their success.

8. They accept mediocrity.

9. They don't practice.

Remember success breeds success. Once you get goal setting down, you will be surprised at how contagious it can be to yourself and your business.

Winners run with winners. You will rise to the level of your peer group. If you surround yourself with positive people, you will become positive. If you hang out with non-producing, negative people, that is exactly what you will be and exactly where you will stay.

The sales profession is a noble one. We are well rewarded for the effort and result that we put in and achieve. If it were easy, everybody would be doing it. As sales professionals, we are a special breed of people.

Imagine yourself as the CEO and sole employee of your own corporation. You are in the personal services business. You provide your expertise. Wouldn't it make sense to be the best that you can be, just like Michael Jordan?

Decide for yourself if this is what you want to do. If not, find something else. If it is, then decide that you are going to put in 110%.

Sometimes we know we should be doing something productive, like making cold calls. But we do not feel like it. We know we should call a prospect to take them to the next step in the sales process, but we do not feel like it.

President Lyndon Johnson said, "Yesterday is not ours to recover, but tomorrow is ours to win or to lose."

Do not worry about what has happened in the past. Focus on what is going to happen today and tomorrow.

Chapter 16: BONUS
25 Proven Ways To Increase Sales Now

1. Create a 15 second commercial about what you do.
This commercial focuses on the benefits that you bring to a prospect. It **clearly** communicates your service and what your client can expect. Script it out word for word, test it and do not be afraid to make changes to fine-tune it. This is what I say...

"I'm Chris Randolph and I'm the president of The Sales Edge. We conduct workshops, seminars and coaching sessions that help sales professionals master what to say, how to say it, when to say it, who to say it to, and we help them identify why they want to become more successful."

Your commercial is simply an introduction of yourself and it is designed to cause someone to say, "Tell me more". A successful sales professional will share what they do with any and everyone that they come into contact with. Also, make sure that all of your friends, neighbors and relatives know exactly what you do. You never know who your friends or relatives know or may come across.

2. Write out your goals (only the ones you want to achieve).
You need to identify and write out your goals to give them life. You must review them every day. Create different categories of goals. They could be career, financial, personal, and even relationship goals. A 4-step structure for setting your goals looks like this:

1.   Identify the reason for why you want to achieve this goal

2.   Be specific, write your goal down and put a date for completion

3.   Create an action plan

4.   Implementation

In fact, if you want to have all of your goals achieved, you must use the GIAP process; the 11-step goal setting and achieving process that virtually guarantees you will achieve any goal that you set.

3. Write in a journal.

Have you ever written down a great idea on a scrap of paper and then could not find it or remember it? Keep all your thoughts, ideas and goals in a journal. This will create a permanent record that you can always refer back to.

Never lose that one great idea that might change the rest of your life because you misplaced the scrap of paper you wrote it on.

Writing in a journal also helps you clarify your thoughts and make them clearer. Then when you have written that thought down, you can go back over it and decide the next step; refinement or implementation.

4. Create a testimonial book

People buy from people that they like and trust. They also tend to ask for references. Create a binder that showcases you and the quality of work and service you provide. Put picture of yourself and your family as well as thank you letters, testimonials and feedback forms.

Start gathering these things now. It is an invaluable tool. Carry this binder wherever you go. It shows prospects and clients that you are a real person. Try to use a nice leather binder and place all of these documents in clear plastic sheets. Use high quality sheet protectors to place all of these documents.

5. Always be on time.

Showing up on time is a reflection on your character. Never make a prospect wait for you. You must allow for things that can delay you, like traffic. Plan out your time in getting there.

Do things like put gas in your car after work or on the weekends. This will save you time if you are on the way to an appointment and the gauge is on 'E'.

One of the best tools that I use to help get me to my appointments on time is my navigation system. It shows me (and talks to me, too!) how to get to where I need to and how long it is going to take me to get there. If I miss a turn, it gets me back on the right track.

6. Plan your day everyday
There are 144,000 minutes in a day. Most experts, including myself, prescribe using 1% of the day to plan the other 99%. This works out to 14 minutes a day. By planning your day, you will have steps that you can follow and keep yourself on track. Your daily plan is the road map to your success.

Do the most important things on your list first. Get them knocked out of the way. You should also tackle the unpleasant tasks as soon as possible.

7. Dress for Success
Wear the best that you can afford. You do not have to buy a lot of it. Just enough that will give the impression of success. You should always look the part of the knowledgeable and confident professional. What's more important is that your clothes are clean and look sharp. It is also the way you carry yourself. And for men, make sure your shoes are clean and shined.

8. Carry cologne and mouthwash with you.
Also, always use a deodorant. An offensive odor will always turn a prospect off. You should always smell your best. Use at least the mouthwash before you walk into a prospect's office. And do not overdo the cologne or perfume.

9. Send out 5 e-mails a day.
Imagine if you were to send out 5 e-mails a day to potential clients. These e-mails would be follow-up e-mails and/or info

e-mails. An E-mail can be as good as a phone call, sometimes better. If you send out 5 e-mails a day, you would make 25 contacts a week, 100 a month, and 1200 a year. It is another form of keeping in touch. When is the last time you contacted or stayed in touch with 1200 people a year?

10. Create an e-mail newsletter

An E-mail newsletter is a highly efficient method to keep your name in front of your prospects and clients. Your newsletter should have useful information and the latest news about you, your company or your industry. Send out a newsletter that reminds your clients and prospects who you are and what you can do for them. For a great resource, check out *www.constantcontact.com* for creating and maintaining your newsletter.

11. Hire an assistant.

Figure out what you are worth an hour. To do this, take your annual gross and divide it by 12 months, and then divide that by 160 hours. The answer will give you your hourly wage. If you come up with anything higher than $30 an hour, you need to hire an assistant.

Your new assistant can handle all of your paperwork and administrative details so you can spend your time selling and concentrating on generating business.

12. Exercise before you start the workday.

Exercise for at least 15 to 30 minutes before you start your day. It can be as strenuous or as easygoing as you like. Besides the obvious health and weight benefits, you get substantial mental benefits too, you will be more alert and your level of concentration will be higher.

It gets your blood pumping, it wakes you up quicker and your mind will come online quicker. You can also use this time to go over your day.

13. Use a prospect management system.
Nothing loses you more money than misplacing a prospect's number, or forgetting to call a prospect back. Track your prospects with a system. You can use index cards in conjunction with a recipe box.

There are also computer software systems that will do the job. It can range from something as simple as Microsoft Outlook to programs like Act or Goldmine.

Whatever you use, make sure you use something that will track and remind you of your phone calls and appointments. It is well worth the investment of time and money.

14. Send thank you cards.
I send every prospect I visit a "thank you" card. You can buy postcards with the postage already on them from the post office. Everyday, when I get back to the office, I pull out my appointments from the previous day.

I send everyone that I met a post card with a short, personalized handwritten message. It gives a great impression, sets you apart from everyone else and gives you the opportunity to reiterate key points from your meeting that you would like to stress again.

15. Use a telephone headset.
If you are a sales professional, you must invest in a telephone headset for yourself. This tool is an absolute must for every sales professional. It keeps your hands free so you can write and take good notes comfortably.

You can buy them for as little as about $20 for a simple setup to $200 with all the bells and whistles. It all depends on your budget, how much time you spend on the phone, and how comfortable you want to be.

16. Ask for referrals.

It is largely agreed among sales people that a referral is an easier sale to close. But why do salespeople hesitate to ask for referrals?

We do this because we are afraid to ask and we are afraid of rejection. This is because salespeople usually ask in a manner that causes them to say no. Typical salespeople usually say, "If you know anyone who can use my service, please have them give me a call."
This is what I say,

> *"I'm growing my business in Southern California. As you know, I work heavily with referrals. A good referral for me is a business owner, sales manager or network-marketing leader with 6 or more people on their team that wants to increase their production. Think about companies that you have worked for in the past, companies that you do business with or would like to do business with. Can you think of anyone that fits this description?"*

17. Hand out your business card to 5 people a day.

A business card is inexpensive but can have great value. Your card should describe what you do. If you hand out a card to 5 people a day, that is 25 a week, 100 a month, 1200 people a year that would have your card. This is over and above what you are already doing.

If you handed out your card to 1200 people every year, by how much would your business increase?
By the way, when you give out your card, make it your goal to get theirs back in return.

18. 4-4-4 Formula

This formula is deceptively simple. It asks you to do three things 4 times a year, once every quarter. The top professionals do these activities. They know that sometimes it is harder to stay at the top than it is to get there. They realize that they must find ways to keep the edge and stay sharp in their game.

1.   Purchase at least 4 books on selling, personal development, motivation or business a year and read them at least once a quarter.

2.   Purchase at least 4 audio programs on selling, personal development, motivation, or business a year and listen to them in your car as often as you can, for example everyday!

3.   Attend 4 live seminars on selling, personal development, motivation or business a year.

Do these every year and your results will improve year after year.

19. Hire a sales and success coach
A coach will help you identify and fine-tune your goals, create an action plan for you to achieve them and hold you accountable for the fulfillment of them.

A coach will help you move along the path to a greater level of achievement and success. We believe so strongly in the power of coaching that The Sales Edge offers an introductory session, valued at $200, absolutely free. This allows you to experience the power of coaching for yourself. Simply send an email to *info@thesalesedge.biz* with "Coaching" in the subject line.

We will hone you skills, help you improve you performance, achieve balance and you will build a thriving book of business.

20. Believe in your product/service/company
For you to sell your product, you have to sell yourself on it first. This is much easier if you represent a solid product at a fair price, backed by a reputable company. The company does not have to be big to be reputable. A good company would treat employees and clients like the valuable resources that they are.

If you currently do not work for such a company, find another one. You will sell better when you do.

21. Spend time with your family.

If you are too busy to spend time with family and friends, something is not right. Our work gives us rewards. One of these should be spending quality time with our family. It makes the hard work that we put in justifiable.

22. Make one more call before you walk out the door.

Making that last call before you leave can bring dividends many times over. You could leave a message or your prospect could even be there! Imagine if you did this everyday. You would make an extra 5 calls a week, 20 a month, 240 extra calls a year! If you make an extra 240 calls this year, how much would your business grow?

23. Model top producers in your industry.

Find out what the top producers in your company and your industry are doing to get those fantastic results and do the same thing. If you can model what they are doing, you will get a similar result.

24. Identify your industry's buying cycle.

The buying cycle is a period of time before a client needs to replace their product because of technological advances, desires or other reasons. For example, in California, the average person replaces their vehicles every 3 to 4 years.

If you worked at an auto dealership, my first suggestion would be to contact customers from 3 to 5 years ago and talk to them about replacing their current automobiles. If you contacted 5 customers a day, that is 25 a week, 100 a month, and 1200 a year. How much do you think you will increase your income if you contacted 1200 previous customers a year?

25. Sell benefits not features.

Features are the characteristics of a product or service. The benefit is what a client gets out of using the product or service.

People buy because of what a product will do for them and nothing else. Make a list of all the possible benefits your client will get if they purchase your product. When you have done this, tell your prospect about them. People buy benefits.

Final Thought:
It is my goal to share with you the techniques, skills and strategies that give the successful sales professional the edge. I urge you to implement the tools in this book. Happy selling and best in success!

Printed in the United States
54202LVS00005B/415-483